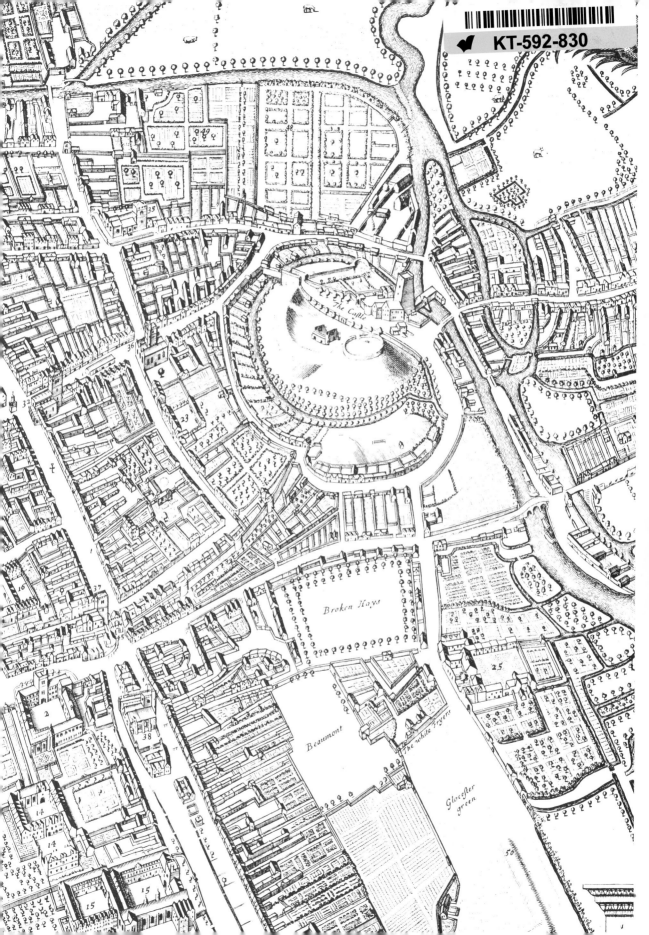

The Castle

Broken Hays

Beaumont

The white Fryers

Glocester green

The Buildings of Oxford

'The river valley is plunged in shadow, and all looks rather dismal. Then as you wait, perhaps with a shiver in the wind, a patch of sunshine breaks through the clouds and sweeps westward up the Thames. Over the opposite hills it goes, like a scythe among the trees, and across the dull suburbs of the city. A factory is momentarily illuminated, the humdrum pattern of a housing estate, a mass of red-brick terraces, the glass geometry of a school, until the beam lands at last upon the ancient centre of Oxford. Instantly something like a vision shines out of the valley. The towers, spires and pinnacles of the city, honey-gold and tightly packed, leap suddenly from the shadows as though they are floodlit. All is sudden etched intricacy – chiselled, elaborate, vertical – a cluster of golden objects picked out in theatrical silhouette.'

Jan Morris, 1965

Opposite
The coat of arms of the City of Oxford from the wooden panel dated 1577.
Town Hall, Oxford

The end papers are taken from the aerial map of Oxford published 1675 by David Loggan. North is at the bottom of the map.

The Buildings of Oxford

Anthony F. Kersting
and
John Ashdown

B. T. BATSFORD LTD
LONDON

First published 1980
Reprinted 1983
Copyright text John Ashdown 1980
Copyright Photographs Anthony F. Kersting 1980
Printed in Great Britain by The Pitman Press Ltd
for the Publishers B. T. Batsford Ltd,
4 Fitzhardinge Street, London W1H 0AH

ISBN 0 7134 0138 9

Contents

Preface and Acknowledgements

This book is concerned with the townscape and buildings of the historic centre of Oxford – the historic buildings of the town, University and colleges. The majority of the photographs were taken recently, to illustrate the townscape and architecture of Oxford as it exists in the late 1970s. Where this has not been possible, or desirable, an older illustration has been chosen. The appearance of Oxford's historic buildings has undergone a remarkable change in the last twenty-five years. The establishment in 1957 of the Oxford Historic Buildings Fund brought into collective focus a great work of repair and cleaning. In the seventeen years that followed the Fund raised nearly £2$\frac{1}{2}$ million outside the University and colleges. The results are impressive. The once decaying, scaly, black stone façades have almost disappeared, to be replaced by new golden stone throughout the City, a process which has also swept away much genuine antiquity. In Oxford the repair of stone, represented by a wholesale replacement of facings, means restoration not conservation. In some cases the result is a triumph, as at the Christ Church Library. In many other cases restoration was certainly necessary, as at the Sheldonian Theatre. The careful treatment of the Radcliffe Camera, however, demonstrates that a moderate conservation approach can achieve fine results too.

The winding up of the Fund has not seen any slackening in the work of repair. Major schemes are in hand at All Souls, Merton, Christ Church and Magdalen. Smaller schemes are always to be seen in progress throughout Oxford on university, college and church buildings. This process of constant renewal is not a new one, and it is often the more recent stone facing or refacings that have decayed. Therefore, externally, and with obvious major exceptions such as the late fourteenth-century fabric at New College, the eye sees restored masonry. 'Sharp is the arris as the mason recently left it.' So much for the philosophical problems of the antiquary. The average eye can see only the great physical beauty of the results, which make up one of the masterpieces of the European architectural heritage.

It would be a mistake, all the same, to consider Oxford as just forming a collection of fine historic buildings. It is true that Oxford and Cambridge contain the only major groups of medieval academic and university buildings still existing and used for their original purposes, and that the subsequent growth of the University in the post-medieval period and more recent times, has created one of the greatest architectural experiences of the British Isles. But Oxford, with its finely displayed historic fabric, is not a museum of architecture nor a tourist town. It is a living city and continues to be a modern trading town containing a world-famous university. At the same time it remains the administrative and leisure centre for its region, and has become a centre for the making of books and the manufacture of motor vehicles. Within the very tight constraints imposed by geography Oxford has managed to maintain its balance in the twentieth century.

We wish warmly to acknowledge the assistance of the many people in Oxford who made it possible to take the photographs that follow. The bursars of the colleges and their staff must be singled out as a group for particular thanks. We also wish to thank the librarians and custodians of individual rooms who bore kindly with us; the curators and Surveyor to the University of Oxford; the Oxford Union Society; the clergy of the Cathedral and parish churches; the City of Oxford, and personal friends.

We also wish to thank Edith Gollnast for drawing the plan of Oxford and the decorative headpieces, and Shirley Knapp for typing the first manuscript. Any work on Oxford must borrow from those gone before and this debt is acknowledged with gratitude.

A. F. K. and J. A. 1978

An Introduction to the Buildings of Oxford

The common seal of the City of Oxford, 1191–1662

Historical Introduction

Oxford, lying among low hills, sits beside the river Thames at the centre
Southern England. As a city, Oxford has become a world academic centre
account of its historic, and contemporary, University. As a modern city
fulfils three major roles. Oxford remains the administrative, shopping, so
and leisure focus of Oxfordshire and its region; it houses a major indust
complex, now forming a part of the Midlands motor vehicle industry; an
retains its University, together with one of the largest concentrations
historic buildings in England. Any one of these roles would be satisfact
enough for most small towns with a population of some 140,000.

The narrow, raised and well-drained plateau of gravel situated between
rivers Thames and Cherwell must always have seemed well protected :
attractive to settlers. While the site of Oxford played little part in the life
Roman Britain, an important ceramic industry flourished east of the Cherw
between Headington and Cowley, and rural settlements existed where to
North Oxford spreads. The first growth of a small town at Oxford came dur
Anglo-Saxon times, stimulated by the improvement of Thames cross
facilities and the beginnings of the monastery of St. Frideswide, tradition
founded as a minster church before 735. The natural importance of the Sa>
roads through Oxford, crossing Southern England north to south and eas
west, would have encouraged the crossroad settlement to expand. Rec
archaeological excavations in St. Aldate's have demonstrated the nature of
first urban life in eighth-century Oxford. The earliest preserved document
reference to a town is in 912, when the *Anglo-Saxon Chronicle* records that K
Edward the Elder claimed Oxford and its region. Oxford, by this time, m
have grown into a fortified frontier town or burgh of the West Saxons agai
the Danes. It is so recorded in the document known as the *Burghal Hidage* wh
describes the frontiers of Wessex in *c.* 920. The archaeological evide
suggests a timber-walled settlement, laid out in a grid-plan of streets. T
town grew rapidly, expanding towards the east, so that by the early eleve
century it was as large as the later medieval stone-walled city.

Following the Norman conquest of England in the 1060s, the 1
government, represented by Robert d'Oilly, erected the Castle, as
overpowering symbol of the change, at the west end of the town. Oxf
flourished under the Normans, its location making it politically important
became perhaps the seventh largest town in the kingdom and gained ci
privileges based on its agricultural and trading wealth.

More religious institutions were attracted to the town at this ti

St. Frideswide's was refounded as an Augustinian Priory by 1122 and the larger Augustinian foundation at Oseney followed in 1129 and was located outside the town on a site west of the Castle. The royal palace of Beaumont was also built outside the walls on the north after 1130.

The growth of town government and the guild merchant was recognised by the granting of royal charters in 1155 and 1199. The second gave rights to collect royal taxation due from the town. It is worth noting that the earliest extant municipal seal in England is that fixed to a charter in which the citizens of Oxford confirmed a grant of land at Medley to Oseney Abbey in 1191.

The growing residence in Oxford of teachers and scholars in the late twelfth century has left little documentary trace, and perhaps was at first largely unnoticed in a busy city used to the existence of important monastic houses. The infant University was essentially an ecclesiastical concern, which gained recognisable status as a *studium generale* in the last decades of the century. The troubles of 1209 resulted in the dispersal of the University and it was not until 1214 that it was re-established, with royal and papal encouragement, and the first Chancellor appointed shortly afterwards. The 1220s saw the arrival of the friars – the Dominicans in 1221 and the Franciscans in 1224 – who built large houses just south of the walled city and had an important influence on the growth of schooling and the status of the University. In 1281 the Cistercians founded Rewley Abbey, situated on the Thames west of the city. While town and gown were heavily dependent on each other, the friction between the townsfolk and the scholars occasionally resulted in riots, notably in 1209, 1298 and 1355. The settlement of these disputes gradually led to the University becoming a dominant party in Oxford's local government.

Oxford was still one of the most prosperous provincial towns in England in the first half of the thirteenth century, a period which saw the erection of a Guildhall in 1229 and the rebuilding in stone of the city walls to a particularly advanced military design in the north-east quarter. However, the general national economic decline of English town life, resulting from the effects of the major plagues and the migration of industries, made Oxford become more dependent on its association with the University in the following century. The political importance of Oxford was now greatly reduced by the expansion of the English kingdom; and the Black Death of 1349 and the subsequent lesser plagues of 1361 and 1369 much reduced the population. The University suffered a temporary decline also, but the increased need for educated men soon reversed this trend. The foundation of New College within the walls in 1379 is indicative both of the need for trained clerks and administrators to run Church and State, and of the availability of building land within the walled town – a facility in earlier years denied to those founding monasteries or friaries.

Originally, the University had had no buildings of its own. Its early meetings, deputations and degree ceremonial were all held at St. Frideswide or at the Church of St. Mary the Virgin, and at the latter the record chests were kept. Similarly, the student of the early years of the University lived in lodgings or in groups in 'halls' under a master. Throughout the Middle Ages the 'undergraduate' was housed largely in the halls and by the early fifteenth century attachment to one was becoming compulsory. The growth of colleges was slow, and they were first intended for Fellows only, as All Souls remains to this day. It was William of Wykeham's College of St. Mary of Winchester, or New College, with its precise statutes, that first linked 'undergraduates' and 'graduates' with Fellows, all together in a common corporate teaching institution. In addition, New College was closely associated with Wykeham's school at Winchester.

The first Oxford Colleges were founded in the second half of the thirteenth century: University (1249), Balliol (1263), Merton (1264), Gloucester (1283) and Durham (1286). Merton has the distinction of having evolved the oldest surviving quadrangle – Mob Quad. Exeter (1314), Oriel (1326), Queen's (1341), Canterbury (1363) and New College (1379) followed during the fourteenth century. The succeeding 130 years, up to the Dissolution of the monastic houses, saw the founding of Lincoln (1427), St. Mary's (1435), St. Bernard's (1437), All Souls (1438), Magdalen (1458), Brasenose (1509), Corpus Christi (1517) and Cardinal College (1525). Canterbury, Durham, Gloucester, St. Bernard's and St. Mary's were monastic colleges and were to disappear at the Dissolution. William of Waynflete's St. Mary Magdalen College and Cardinal Wolsey's Cardinal College followed New College in status and scale of buildings. At the end of the Middle Ages the colleges far outstripped the University in wealth and buildings. Gradually the colleges became the recognised centres for teaching, and control of the University passed to the heads of the colleges.

The academic life of Oxford was too strong to wither away at the English Reformation, an event in which the Oxford reformers had taken a leading part from the 1590s, when Erasmus visited the University. However, the events of the Reformation greatly changed Oxford, administratively and physically. The monastic houses, friaries and monastic colleges were closed and much of their wonderful heritage of architecture was destroyed. Chance saved the church of St. Frideswide's Priory when it became the Cathedral and Collegiate Church of Christ, following Henry VIII's refounding of Cardinal College and the creation of the Oxford Diocese at Oseney in 1542, and its transfer to Christ Church in 1546. Three new colleges were founded in the middle years of the sixteenth century: Trinity (1555) on the site of Durham, St. John the Baptist (1555) on the site of St. Bernard's, and Jesus (1571). The Marian persecutions of the 1550s saw Bishops Latimer and Ridley and Archbishop Cranmer burnt in Broad Street. Academic life certainly faltered in an age of uncertainty as the almost total destruction of the central University Library housed in Duke Humfrey's room over the Divinity School demonstrates. However, Elizabeth I granted a new charter to the University in 1563. Town and gown wrangled over the government of the town at length in this period also. However, the City was beginning to flourish again and the first half of the seventeenth century was a time of prosperity. This was based on a resurgence of Oxford's consumer trade. Immigrants came as apprentices, the food and drink trade flourished, and the road carriers and the Thames were again busy. A good water supply was created from Hinksey in 1615, the streets were paved, and the result of the great rebuilding or refurbishing of town houses that was then carried out is still evident today. Oxford was granted a new Charter of

Incorporation by King James I in 1605, and the University's statutes were revised under Chancellor Laud in 1636.

The seventeenth century also saw a revival in the fortunes of the central university institutions. Sir Thomas Bodley began the reconstruction of the Duke Humfrey Library in 1598 and it was able to reopen in 1602. The library building was expanded, and the New Schools were erected between 1613–20. Classical Renaissance architectural design had at last reached Oxford, though hardly understood at first and used as a decorative treatment added to late-Gothic façades. Two new colleges were founded, Wadham (1610) and Pembroke (1624), and both remained faithful to the Oxford Gothic, except in detail. New quadrangles were designed with three storeys of residential sets, and many chapels were embellished with glorious painted glass made by the immigrant van Linges from Emden in Lower Saxony. A Physic or Botanic Garden was established in 1621 by Magdalen Bridge.

The Civil War again demonstrated the importance of Oxford as a political centre in a Southern English context, with its declaration as King Charles I's headquarters after the Royalists' failure to take London in 1642. The college buildings made an adequate background for the Court and the King. Safe behind substantial new gun-protecting earthworks, the City was twice besieged before surrendering in June 1646. All university activity was suspended for the duration of the war. The frustrations of the troubled middle years of the century were succeeded at the Restoration by a period of academic activity, and for a short while Oxford was the centre of European scientific research. The Restoration period also saw the erection of the Sheldonian Theatre, Christopher Wren's first major building, fully classical in design, and the establishment of the first Ashmolean Museum adjoining it. University printing was finally established under Dean Fell and by the 1690s a true university press existed under the control of Delegates. By 1712 the Press could occupy fine new premises next to the Sheldonian, the Clarendon Building, designed by Hawksmoor.

The eighteenth century was a time of dignified progress, but no great academic activity, while the City, although again provincial, prospered. Worcester College was founded in 1714, on the site of Gloucester Hall and College, and Hertford College, less successfully, in 1740. Major schemes involving the construction of new college buildings were undertaken at Queen's and All Souls. Other grand schemes remained largely on paper. The munificent bequests of John Radcliffe, physician to the royal family, who died in 1714, eventually resulted in the University gaining its dominant circular library, the Radcliffe Camera (which opened in 1749), and the Radcliffe Observatory, completed in 1794. The Radcliffe Infirmary, also the work of the Radcliffe Trustees, opened in 1770. The 1770s saw a major series of city improvements: the markets were removed from the streets into a new covered market; constricting town gates were demolished; a new road was constructed to the west through the Castle; and Magdalen Bridge was rebuilt in grand style. The narrow boat canal linking Oxford with the coal and manufactures of the Midlands reached the City in 1790. This, and improved turnpike roads, marked the beginning of the end of the local economy and started processes in

marketing which still continue today. The railway, held at bay for a wh
reached Oxford in 1844. The gas works and gas street lighting arrived by 18

Oxford in 1801 had a population of 12,000, with many people living
conditions of extreme congestion and poverty in the central city a
Consequently, when Oxford began to grow in the 1820s, contrary to the us
pattern it was the poor rather than the rich who needed to move out to the n
fringe suburbs of St. Ebbe's, Jericho, Walton Manor, St. Clement's a
further afield, Summertown. The growth of Jericho is also associated with
canal and the move, completed by 1830, of university printing to Wal
Street. Sanitary conditions in the new suburbs (as elsewhere), were far fr
perfect and the national outbreaks of cholera visited Oxford in 1832 and 18
A significant pointer for the future was the first unified estate development
St. John's College adjoining St. Giles. Here in Beaumont Street, St. John Str
and Beaumont Buildings the College from 1824 developed a balanced hierar
of new housing in terraces, designed in a late Georgian style, grading fr
polite Bath stone to practical Headington Quarry red brick.

By 1851 the population had risen to 27,000, but it was not until the build
of Park Town after 1854 and the development of the Walton Manor
Norham Manor Estates in North Oxford for St. John's College after 1860, t
many of the richer tradespeople and clergy were able to move out to subur
houses. The North Oxford Victorian suburb was first built with houses in
fashionable High Victorian Gothic manner, a great contrast to the restrai
Classic of Park Town or the small Georgian vernacular houses of the f
nineteenth-century expansion. After 1880 the distinct character of the No
Oxford Victorian suburb was continued in a quieter Oxford brick-and-st
style, following the decision of the 1877 Royal Commission to allow Fellow
colleges to marry. While North Oxford was not created by this change in
university rules, its later development was greatly affected by it.

While Keble College (1870), the only major foundation of the ninetee
century, was appropriately sited in a suburban situation, many of the cen
colleges made substantial additions to their buildings in this period. Th
included Hertford, refounded in 1874. Of great consequence for the future
the creation after 1879 of new establishments for women to attend
University. That was the year in which Lady Margaret Hall and Somerv
Hall were founded. The University itself also greatly expanded its build
programme, notably with the construction of the new museums:
University Galleries, now the Ashmolean Museum (1841), the Univers
Museum (1855) and the Pitt Rivers Museum (1885); and with the erection
the new Examination Schools in High Street from 1876. By 1900
population had reached 49,000 and the University had evolved as a mod
institution.

In 1913 W. R. Morris assembled the prototype Morris-Oxford motor
in a car-hire garage in Longwall Street, under the shadow of the medie
city-wall. Almost at a stroke, a major component of modern Oxford was add
though fortunately demand for space made necessary from the first a mov
the village of Cowley. Morris Motors were joined by the Pressed St
Company in 1926. By 1939 the population of Oxford had risen to 96,000

modern suburbs of Marston, Headington, Cowley and Donnington had grown around the older villages to house the workers of industrial Oxford.

The University has continued to grow in the twentieth century. The number of colleges has increased during the course of the century from 22 to St. Peters (1929), Nuffield (1937), St. Catherine's (1963), and Wolfson (1965) being major foundations. In addition, St. Edmund Hall, founded in the 1200s, achieved college status in 1957. To these must be added the five permanent private halls attached to the University, and other colleges and halls enjoying this status. A great number of other private educational bodies have also grown up in Oxford, making use of the worldwide fame of its name. The Oxford Polytechnic is situated on Headington Hill, and the hospitals and medical schools of Oxford have grown into a complex of important institutions, now dominated by the huge white monster of the John Radcliffe hospital at Headington. Closely associated with the University is the growth of book-selling and publishing. The fame of the University and the beauty of its buildings and those of the colleges has led to an uncomfortable increase in all types of visitors to Oxford.

The twentieth century has treated historic Oxford kindly, except in one respect, that, ironically, being pollution from motor vehicles. Considerable resources have been spent on repairing and restoring the historic fabric and it is good to recall the total absence of damage during the Hitler war. Even the motor vehicle has lost battles: the welcome failure to build the inner ring road across Christ Church Meadow has been the greatest victory against it. The successful creation of a complete ring of outer by-passes has diverted the damaging through-traffic and enabled balanced traffic management to improve the living and working conditions of the central city.

Oxford is still a small city, with a population of some 140,000 within the built-up area. Unrestrained by town planning policies, Oxford would have grown considerably after 1945, for Oxford is a magnet in today's world. Fortunately for historic Oxford, chance, geography and geology have influenced the location of the nineteenth- and twentieth-century suburban expansion. The centre of Oxford sits astride its low plateau of gravel, enclosed by the wide flood plain meadows of the rivers Thames and Cherwell. Common sense has resulted in these open spaces' remaining free from development and Oxford has remained in close touch with its countryside. Restraint of Oxford's growth is now a national planning aim and a 'Green Belt' policy has reinforced the natural constraints at the City's extremities.

Like the rest of England, Oxford has as a result of social changes altered a great deal in the twentieth century. The survival of its historic buildings is impressive, however, particularly in the eastern half of the City. Losses of such buildings have been small, but Oxford has not been able to avoid the inevitable changes of modern retailing and the invasion of national companies with corporate images. Major retailing interests have been erosive in Oxford as elsewhere, but fortunately the intricate nature of the townscape has resisted destruction. The City Council's Westgate shopping centre and multi-storey car park, similarly destructive of an older Oxford, is well planned in relation to the functioning of the City in the twentieth century. Oxford has not escaped the creation of municipal open spaces and car parks achieved in the name of slum clearance. The nineteenth-century suburb of St. Ebbe's, and the medieval and later suburb of St. Thomas' lying on the south-west quarter of the City, have been almost totally obliterated, good and bad together, for planned renewal and traffic improvements, the latter now almost overtaken by events. It must not be forgotten, however, that St. Ebbe's was dominated by the gas works with its giant cylinder holders, the sight of which is now an almost forgotten memory. St. Ebbe's will grow again with new housing over the next ten years, bringing town life right back to the edge of the business and historic centre.

The Setting of Oxford

The best way to begin to understand a town or city is to stand a little way off and look at it from outside. This is possible at Oxford, and the motorist from the south-west and south on reaching the ring road roundabouts at once sees the City's skyline over or through a maze of Generating Board pylons. The motorist from the London direction, however, can no longer enjoy the view his eighteenth-century counterpart saw, and Magdalen Bridge and the High Street are reached almost too abruptly. Travellers from the British Rail station, having glided by a good view of the City's skyline seen over the green foreground of the gas works site, may later be excused for thinking that they have alighted at the wrong destination as they gaze at the squalor of the station area. The view from the station entrance demonstrates how little modern Oxford collectively cares for its environment or is able to create a new environment outside the University.

Wonderful viewpoints looking down to Oxford do remain, but they have to be searched out. The enchanting long-distance vignette seen from the Oxford Preservation Trust field on Boars Hill, requires bright sunlight and clouds to be at its best and at such times can be stunningly beautiful: an eighteenth-century stone town lying in the valley flanked by green hillsides; the twentieth century invisible. The descent of South Park on Headington Hill in the morning can also be very rewarding. The best panorama of the ancient and modern City may be seen, however, from Raleigh Park, over North Hinksey village on the western hills. North Oxford, with its Victorian suburb, lies to the left, and Cowley with its works lies to the right before the Chiltern scarpe. In front spreads the spired and towered skyline of the historic City, above the modern Osney industrial estate (where the towers of the medieval Oseney Abbey once rose), and above squats the white bulk of the John Radcliffe Hospital at Headington. No illusion here: ancient and modern are displayed together. In the winter the foreground meadows can be a wide flood of enclosing water about the City: a sight which graphically illustrates why the urban limits have stopped where they do.

The skyline of the historic City consists of spires, towers, pinnacles, domes, pyramids and square blocks. The dominant colours are those of the golden stone, cleaned and repaired over the last decade, and the lush setting of trees.

The Historic Buildings of Oxford

The visual character and townscape of a historic city derive both from the appearance of its ancient and contemporary buildings and from the way they and the spaces between them are used. The visual character of Oxford is made by the contrast of monumental university and college buildings with the more humble historic houses of the town, placed within the complex fabric of the City's streets and lanes. What complex and unique groups of buildings these are! Today Oxford and Cambridge contain the only major survivals of medieval academic and university buildings in use for their original purposes. The growth of the University in the post-medieval period, and in more recent times, has created one of the great architectural experiences of these islands. The enclosing medieval city-wall can still be followed on the ground and the early rectangular street layout remains largely in use. The historic buildings of the University and colleges are situated, with certain notable exceptions, in the eastern half of the ancient walled City. Modern commercial activity has concentrated therefore in the centre and western half, in touch with the western suburbs which have always contained the industrial quarter of the town.

The complex nature of the Oxford townscape can be seen by ascending one of the three public viewpoints: the Sheldonian cupola, the tower of St. Mary the Virgin Church, or Carfax tower. From these high places the relationship of college quadrangles to narrow medieval domestic housing plots, and the towers, pinnacles and roofs, can be observed. The townscape of towers, spires and domes can, of course, be enjoyed in constantly changing views at all levels within the City. The walk on the north side of the High Street, from Magdalen Bridge to Carfax, unfolds a changing townscape of tall ascents among the mix of monument and foil, grand buildings and humble vernacular ones.

The predominant historic building materials reflect the status of Oxford's builders and the town's location among Corallian rag-stone hills, within reach of fine stones of the Jurassic limestone belt to the north. Once established, the stone-using tradition has continued to the present day, the local medieval sources of Wheatley, Headington and Taynton having given way in time to Bath (in the late eighteenth century), to Clipsham in Rutland (after 1876) and more recently to France (from 1974). Historic town buildings used oak timber frames while fashion decreed these were to be displayed, changing to lighter, plastered, flat fronts at a later date. Absent in Oxford, with minor exceptions, is eighteenth-century brick, and in the nineteenth century brick was at first confined to the growing suburbs until Keble College introduced polychrome brickwork for college use.

It may be helpful, as an aid to understanding them, to divide the historic buildings of Oxford into three classes: firstly those of the town, secondly those built by the University as a central institution, and thirdly those erected by the self-governing colleges. In the central area of Oxford over 900 buildings, ranging in date from the mid-eleventh century to the early twentieth century, are included on the statutory list of buildings of special architectural or historic interest compiled by the Government.

The Buildings of The Town

The City of Oxford had already enjoyed over 450 years of continuous growth before the University began its own development. Few standing buildings remain from the early Middle Ages, the churches, the Castle and the city-wall being the most notable. The late Anglo-Saxon tower of St. Michael's Church, originally part of the Northgate in Cornmarket, and the keep-like St. George's

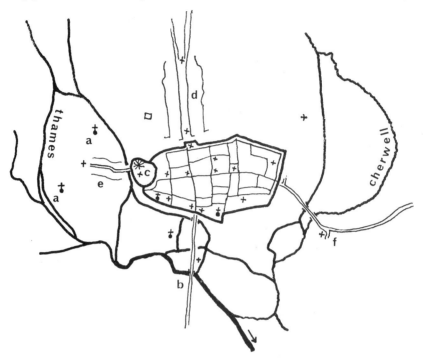

Medieval Oxford located between the rivers Thames and Cherwell.
a *Abbey.* **b** *Folly Bridge.* **c** *Castle.* **d** *St. Giles.* **e** *St. Thomas.* **f** *St. Clements.*

Tower of the early Norman castle, built of time-resistant ragstone-rubble from the Corallian hills surrounding Oxford, represent the oldest monuments. The defensive city-walls reconstructed in the thirteenth century are also an impressive survival. There was originally, in part, a double wall system with projecting semi-circular bastion towers. Seen at their best in the grounds of New College, traces of wall and bastions survive around the whole circuit and can be perambulated by the perceptive visitor.

The medieval parish churches are, or were, sited largely on the main-road axis of the town and at the cardinal points in the first suburbs. Of the survivors, or their rebuilt successors, eight remain in parish use, two are now college chapels and two others are used as college libraries. With its elaborate crypt, St. Peter-in-the-East, now the library of St. Edmund Hall, is the major Romanesque parish church of Oxford, and may be contrasted with the church of St. Giles, standing at the northern extremity of its extra-mural suburb, which contains good Early-English work. St. Peter-in-the-East can also be

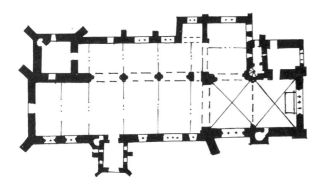

ipared with the elaborate Romanesque parish church in the nearby village Iffley. The major surviving medieval church in the City is that which ;inally belonged to the Augustinian Priory of St. Frideswide. It was orbed into Cardinal Wolsey's Cardinal College, and since 1546 has been the hedral and Collegiate Church of Christ in Oxford, or simply Christ Church. s, alas, the only remaining fabric of the monastic and friary churches of lieval Oxford. The loss of these was considerable, but Christ Church is a utiful Romanesque church begun in the 1180s, extended with chapels in the owing century, and constantly embellished since. Its history has been ntful, with the inevitable losses through change and destruction, but the ir-roof vaulting, rebuilt around 1500, and the fine series of glass windows, outstanding treasures.

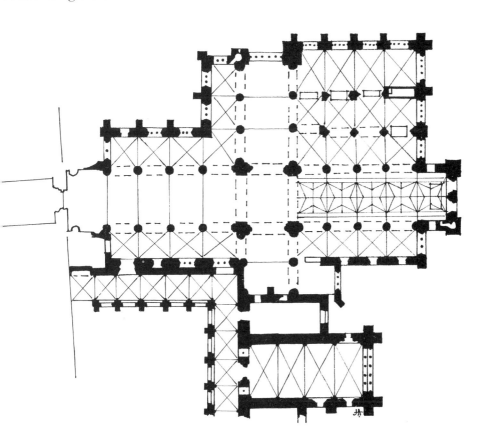

The history of St. Mary the Virgin Church in High Street is as much that of the University as that of the town and the strands of events of both are tightly woven together in it. As it now stands, it is a fine example of Perpendicular Gothic of the second half of the fifteenth century, with its earlier tower and spire.

The historic houses of Oxford, together with the remains of the medieval academic lodging halls, are to be sought scattered among the colleges and commercial buildings of the City. Well-preserved groups of houses will be found in High Street, Merton Street, Ship Street, Holywell Street, Pembroke Street and St. Giles. The Golden Cross Inn off Cornmarket, 28 Cornmarket Street and 126 High Street, can be singled out as individual late-medieval houses of merit. Remains of the academic halls tend to be less evident, but the fourteenth-century Tackley's Inn at 106–7 High Street (now Abbey National Building Society), with an open hall and a medieval vaulted under-croft, is the major survivor.

The houses of the sixteenth- and seventeenth-century town include multi-storeyed oak-framed structures, while others are built in the Cotswold rubble-stone tradition. Unlike London, where seventeenth-century building regulations outlawed external timber construction, Oxford continued to build timber-framed structures well into the nineteenth century. Older houses were often re-fronted with rendered flat façades. Such façades easily mislead the observer in the street, for a wealth of earlier interior fittings, such as fireplaces, wall paintings, panelling, plasterwork and interior structures, as well as vaults and roofs, remain hidden behind later frontages.

The Buildings of The University

The origin of the specialist buildings evolved to house the University's teaching, meetings, records and books may be sought at the parish church of St. Mary the Virgin. Here, in an earlier structure than the existing Perpendicular church, the ceremonial and teaching of the early University was undertaken and record and other chests kept. The erection of the two-storey building, now called the Old Congregation House, was realised in the 1320s. It is a separate structure standing north of the chancel of St. Mary's, and consisted of a vaulted meeting room with a library chamber above, the whole solely for university use. Unlike the later endowed colleges, the University made slow progress in increasing its accommodation. The projected Schola Theologica, or Divinity School, was begun shortly after 1420 on a site just within the northern city-wall. It had a slow building history involving changes of design and a decision to add the Duke Humfrey Library above the lower room, duplicating the arrangements, on a larger scale, that existed at the Old Congregation House. The building was not completed until the 1480s, but it is a masterpiece with a magnificent lierne vault over the Divinity School and the spacious oak-roofed reading room above. A block of two-storey teaching schools was also erected in 1440, adjoining the Divinity School. These

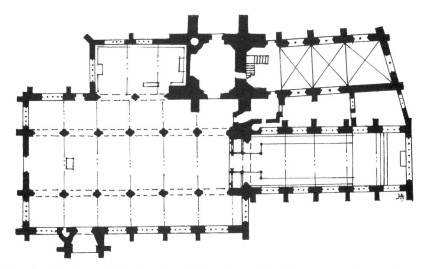

Parish church of St. Mary the Virgin and the University's medieval Congregation House. Plan 1:500.

fifteenth-century buildings form the key to the subsequent development of the University's own buildings south of Broad Street. Progress was slow and had to await the end of the lean Elizabethan years.

In the last decade of the sixteenth century Sir Thomas Bodley set about re-equipping the Duke Humfrey Library. The reconstructed upper room, opened in 1602, was completely re-fitted, stocked and given the exceptional painted armorial decoration to the earlier plain oak roof. From this beginning Bodley guided the creation of a Schools Quadrangle attached to the east end of the Divinity School block. The medieval Schools were demolished and a new three-storey quadrangle built in Oxford's unrelieved late-Perpendicular style between 1613 and 1620. The exception is the great entrance tower, on Catte Street, which, internally to the quad, was given a spectacular classical façade of the Five Orders. At the west end of the Divinity School the Convocation House followed in 1634–7, providing a real parliament chamber for the University. It remains one of the most evocative rooms of seventeenth-century Oxford.

Following the return to normal life after the Civil War, Archbishop Sheldon provided a practical alternative to the use, of which he disapproved, of St. Mary's Church for University ceremonies. His gift in 1663 provided Christopher Wren with the opportunity to design his first major classical building, based on the antique theatre of Marcellus in Rome.

The Sheldonian Theatre was complete by 1669. Robert Streeter's painting of the open sky spans 68 feet of unsupported ceiling and the whole effect was of great contemporary interest. The first home of the Ashmolean Museum was

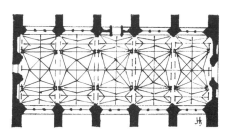

The Divinity School 1424–83. Plan 1:500.

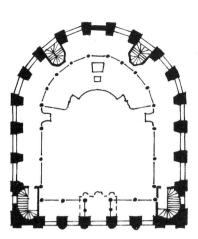

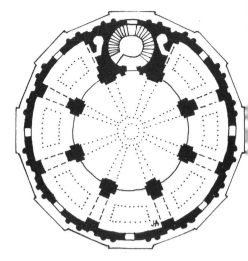

Sheldonian Theatre 1663–9. Plan 1:500.   *Radcliffe Camera 1737–49. Plan 1:500.*

erected close by in 1679–83. Inconveniently, the Theatre also provided accommodation for the new University Press, an arrangement not finally improved until the Clarendon Building was erected as the Printing House in 1712, to a design of Nicholas Hawksmoor. The growth of the University in the eighteenth century is symbolised by the distinctive contribution made by Dr. John Radcliffe's generosity. The Radcliffe Camera or Library, James Gibbs' great domed Classical rotunda, opened in 1749, and has since dominated a typical informal English space created by removing town houses. Today the central group of medieval and Classical buildings, which form the focus of the historic University, is now totally made over to the use of the Bodleian Library. They are linked together by an underground passage and under Broad Street to the New Bodleian book stacks.

The second half of the eighteenth century saw another major Classical building erected by the Radcliffe Trustees. The Radcliffe Observatory, known as the Tower of the Winds, was erected north of St. Giles in open country in 1772–94. Designed by Henry Keene and James Wyatt, it contained an observing room set high in a tower above the observer's house. The Classical tradition continued into the middle years of the nineteenth century. C. R.

Radcliffe Observatory and Observer's House 1772–94. Plan 1:500.

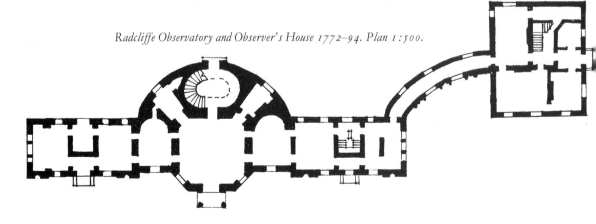

Cockerell's scholarly and monumental Taylor Institute and University Galleries, the latter now known as the Ashmolean Museum, of 1839–45, is unrivalled. The Taylor Institute stands across St. Giles from the Martyrs Memorial of 1841–3, designed by George Gilbert Scott: the confrontation sums up the architectural crisis of the time. The full contrast brought about by the revival of Gothic and the introduction of new constructional materials, can be seen in the central court of the University (Natural History) Museum in Parks Road. Here in 1855–60 Thomas Deane and Benjamin Woodward created a roofed space with a forest of iron columns supporting high whalebone-shaped trusses, under a lattice of glass.

The University has built much in the twentieth century and created an undistinguished campus of workshops and theatres behind the University Museum, quaintly known as the Science Area. Its overcrowded layout does not allow its buildings to be admired. It is worth pondering the complete success of the recent two-storey extension of the Radcliffe Science Library. It lies under the lawn in front of the Deane-and-Woodward Museum. Three major recent complexes elsewhere demand mention, two designed by Leslie Martin: the brick Law Library at St. Cross of 1961–4 and the board-marked concrete of the Department of Zoology and Psychology nearby in South Parks Road of 1971; and finally the unsettling Engineering and Nuclear Physics buildings north of Keble Road.

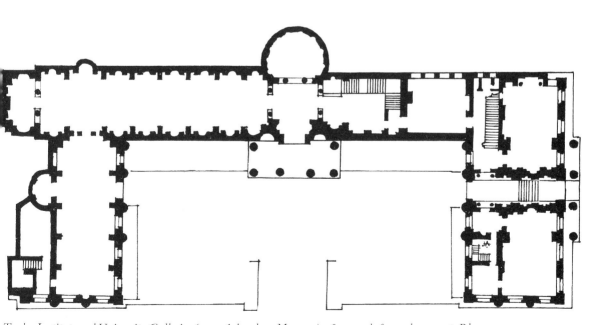

Taylor Institute and University Galleries (now Ashmolean Museum) 1839–45 before enlargement. Plan 1:500.

The Buildings of The Colleges

The first building developments resulting from the founding of residential colleges took place in the early fourteenth century. It was not until the second half of the century, however, that founders were able, at a time of general economic and population decline in Oxford, to purchase large blocks of property for college use, particularly in the eastern half of the ancient walled City. This is well demonstrated by New College where, in the 1370s, streets were closed or diverted, and the college buildings and open grounds replaced the town houses and halls formerly on the site. Even the responsibility of maintenance of a section of the city-wall was taken over by New College. The same process of expansion has taken place ever since. For example at Merton, the Fellows' gardens had replaced house plots by the seventeenth century; at Brasenose and Oriel new quadrangles were created over townhouse plots, facing the High Street in the late nineteenth and early twentieth century. While this process of expansion has continued up to the present, the protection of historic houses by planning law has now changed its emphasis to the conservation of existing buildings, with new buildings fitted into small sites tightly constrained by those already existing.

The earliest quadrangle formed of residential and library accommodation developed, by the accident of necessity, during the first half of the fourteenth century at Mob Quad in Merton College. The formal layout, planning and architectural design found at New College in the 1370s is quite different, and is associated with the Royal Court school of design, which firmly introduced the two-storey closed quadrangle as a basic Oxford planning system. This use of regular quadrangles, to contain the buildings required by the specialised residential communities, intensified the townscape of streets and lanes of Oxford. It created complexes of spaces and gardens accessible from the streets via lodges, but invisible behind buildings and high walls. Generally these 'interior' spaces – quadrangles, courts, cloisters or gardens – do not form through-routes, but give local access only within each college. The slow growth over the centuries of the colleges, placed tightly upon the medieval street-plan, rising sheer from the back of pavements, has resulted in a density of major historic buildings of great beauty.

The standard functional building types found in an Oxford college comprise a gate tower with porter's lodge and warden's accommodation, residential and study rooms, dining hall, kitchen, common rooms, chapel, library, and service and maintenance accommodation, the latter formerly including barns, brewhouses and stabling. To the street or lane are presented impenetrable façades or even blank walls. Entrance to each college is through the lodge or gate house, allowing control by the watchful porter. Originally, the accommodation for the warden was often provided in the tower over the gate house and a fine first-floor room can still remain in this position. The size and internal elevational treatment of the quadrangles have an endless variety, even when account is taken of the repetitive design of Oxford's sixteenth- and seventeenth-century late-Perpendicular Gothic and its Victorian derivatives.

three-storeyed ranges became normal after 1610 and it is well to be aware that many early façades have been heightened since they were first built, or have had elaborated dormer windows added, to allow the roof spaces to accommodate students, since the sixteenth-century reforms. There are striking contrasts to be enjoyed in the quadrangles. Compare the grave cloisters at New College c. 1400), for example, and their early Perpendicular tracery, with Canterbury Quadrangle at St. John's College (1631–6), and its Laudian Classical arcades and frontispieces placed onto a contemporary range of embattled and mullioned Oxford Gothic. To take another example, the eighteenth-century drama of Peckwater Quadrangle at Christ Church, with the great white drums of the library, has a totally Roman impact, so different from that of the multi-coloured brick and stone used at Keble College in the brave new Victorian world. Again, the modern Sir Thomas White Building at St. John's and the recent new quadrangle at Keble may be contrasted with Hertford College's third quadrangle off Holywell or Lincoln College's tight new quadrangles off Bear Lane, south of the High. Here can be seen the careful conservation approach, developed in this second half of the twentieth century.

It is important to understand the planning of the accommodation provided within the ranges round the quadrangles in the older colleges. New College in the last quarter of the fourteenth century had, as we have noted, set the example, on a grand scale, of a carefully planned layout, placing the large-scale elements of the hall and chapel in line. The use of differently sized windows helps the viewer from outside to understand the interior arrangements. The chapel has the larger windows, the hall perhaps a little smaller, in medieval buildings, though a desire for symmetry overrides this consideration at a later date. The smallest windows are the domestic ones of study and bedroom. In the Middle Ages the residential set comprised a large room with study cubicles off it. From the second half of the seventeenth century this arrangement was modified so that a set comprised a large living-study room with two small bedrooms adjoining it. It is valuable to remember that domestic windows can change their appearance over the centuries, and that from the early eighteenth century double-hung sashes have replaced earlier mullion and transomed casements. Internally, the rooms are not accessed by corridors, but form paired groups served by a single staircase.

The dining halls provide a centre for corporate life. It is instructive to contrast the earliest surviving hall, that of the warden at Merton College and strictly his private house, built in 1299 with massive oak trusses supported on crown posts, with Cardinal Wolsey's monster of a room (of 1529) roofed by

Christ Church Hall 1525–9. Plan 1:500.

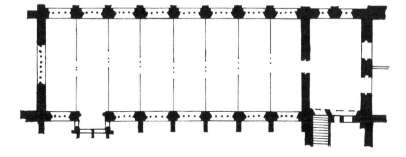

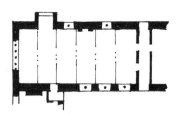

*Corpus Christi College
Hall 1518. Plan
1:500.*

hammer-beam trusses at Christ Church. A fairer contrast would be with the small hall at Corpus Christi of 1518, built by the same craftsmen as those employed at Christ Church. Fine medieval kitchens survive at Christ Church, Lincoln, Magdalen and New College.

The college chapels have always provided for worship and music. They still reverberate with the sound of organ music. They are also rich sources for the observation of fine craftsmanship, the changing taste in design and the philosophy of the treatment of historic monuments. The fittings, furnishings and window glass particularly reflect this latter aspect. The chapels in Oxford provide an unrivalled opportunity to examine in one place decorative window glass, stained and painted, medieval to modern: the work of the unknown masters in the Cathedral, Merton or New College; the van Linges at Lincoln, University, Queen's and Wadham; the work of Price in the eighteenth century at Queen's or of Burne-Jones and Morris again at Christ Church.

The constant renewal of the chapel interiors is well demonstrated by the case of New College. Erected in 1380–6, the walls now support a Victorian roof, replacing an eighteenth-century one; the great reredos with its figures is a restoration, as are the stalls which fortunately retain their medieval misericords. The glass in the chapel is of the eighteenth century, but some of the medieval glass survives in the antechapel, alongside Joshua Reynolds' ethereal west window of *c.* 1780. The twentieth century is represented by the organ and Epstein's graphic white sculpture of Lazarus. An El Greco apostle

New College Chapel and Hall 1480–6. Plan 1:500.

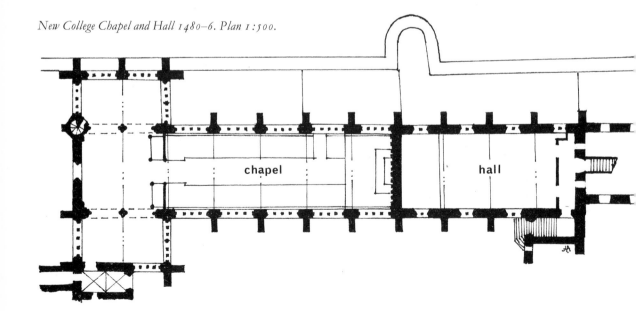

Trinity College Chapel
1691–4. Plan 1:500.

gazes over the altar steps at a portrait of William of Wykeham, the founder.
Wykeham's pastoral staff, a magnificent piece of late fourteenth-century
goldsmith's work is found in a wall case. Evidence of continuity and constant
renewal is everywhere, but the effect is timeless. Trinity College chapel, in total
contrast, is a completely preserved interior of the late seventeenth century with
sumptuous fittings of oak, juniper and limewood, below plasterwork and
paintings. The sixteenth-century alabaster tomb of the founder is placed in a
glazed cupboard to avoid spoiling the effect of the whole. However, it is worth
noting that the organ case is of the mid-twentieth century and does not jar at all.
Three further chapel contrasts only, all Victorian, may be mentioned. At Keble
College, William Butterfield's architectural design and polychrome materials of
1868–82 are equally impressively preserved intact, with the decoration and
fittings of the Oxford Tractarian movement. Rather different and quite
startling at first, is C. E. Kempe's plentiful redecoration in the 1880s of the early
eighteenth-century chapel at Pembroke College. William Burgess's redecoration of the Worcester College chapel of 1864 is even more dramatic.

It is impossible to imagine a university functioning without books, and
each college has its own library. These libraries collectively form an impressive
group and, because they are rarely accessible to the visitor, are little known
internally. The oldest is the late fourteenth-century library room, refitted in the
late sixteenth and early seventeenth centuries, at Merton College. Impressive
medieval-style rooms remain at New College (*c.* 1380), Trinity (*c.* 1420), All
Souls (*c.* 1440) and Corpus Christi (*c.* 1520). To protect the books and
manuscripts from damp, all these rooms were placed at first-floor level. The
dark rooms of the Middle Ages and the early post-medieval period contrast with
the later brilliant showroom–reading rooms, of the late seventeenth and
eighteenth centuries, at Queen's College (*c.* 1695), Christ Church (1720–1770),

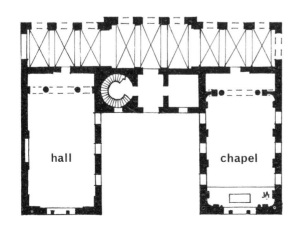

Worcester College Chapel and Hall begun
1720. Plan 1:500.

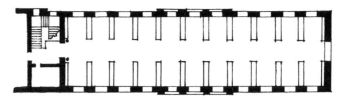

the Codrington at All Souls (1715–50), Worcester (1740) and Oriel (c. 1790). These long, high, but generally narrow rooms reduce the books they contain to insignificance, but the bookcases are equal in scale, with wooden galleries giving access to upper shelves, in the eighteenth-century rooms. Queen's and Christ Church have fine plaster ceilings, but the stall bookcases and the two storey wall cases dominate in the memory, particularly the surprising projecting Baroque entablature carrying the gallery at All Souls. Two of the most recent libraries are interior conversions of parish churches, a welcome use for such problematic buildings of the contemporary inner City. St. Edmund Hall uses the medieval St. Peter-in-the-East (1971) and Lincoln College has recreated the early eighteenth-century interior of All Saints, on The High, as an interior space of wonderful beauty (1975). The most recent college library, however, is the dramatic concrete and glass fortress, completed in 1977, for Wadham College. More than books have to be housed by colleges, and the modern picture gallery at Christ Church provides an exciting home for the collection of Italian paintings and Old Master drawings.

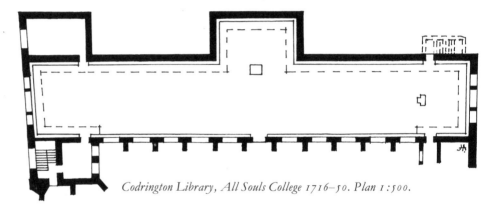

Codrington Library, All Souls College 1716–50. Plan 1:500.

Conclusion

This rapid summary of some of the distinctive features and contrasts of the historic buildings that make up the historic City of Oxford can only serve as an introduction to its rich urban fabric, but it may help to equip the eye of the observer to begin to penetrate its complexity. Mr. Kersting's fine photographs well capture the uniqueness and quality of Oxford in the 1970s. They will enable the visitor to carry away a reminder of its rich heritage. Oxford is now a city full of people as never before in its long history: as a City and University it has been, and is, peopled by a remarkable range of personalities. It remains first and foremost an historic City and University which is to be lived in and enjoyed on foot today.

The Setting

The coat of arms of the University of Oxford

1 The long-distance view: Oxford seen from the Oxford Preservation Trust's fields on Boars Hill

2 *The historic centre of Oxford seen from the air. The mix of grand and foil, monumental quadrangles with minor buildings placed together in a tight, complex but integrated layout is the result of centuries of slow growth*

The Skyline

3 Looking east from the cupola of the Sheldonian Theatre over Hertford College and New College to the green background of Headington Hill

4 Tower, dome and spire over the pinnacles of the Schools Quadrangle as seen from the cupola of the Sheldonian Theatre

The Buildings of The Town and Townscape

The common seal of the City of Oxford after 1682

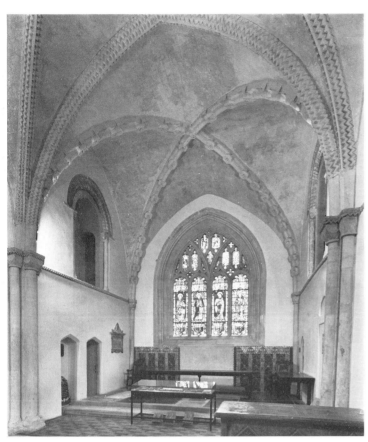

6 FAR LEFT *Carfax tower stands at the centre of Oxford. Only the tower survives from St. Martin's Church, now taken over by the City as a proud belfry and clock-tower*

7 CENTRE *St. George's Tower within Oxford Castle. This tall keep-like structure, built shortly after the Norman Conquest of England, still dominates the Oxford Prison which today occupies the castle precinct. Constructed in resistant coral ragstone rubble, the tower stands above the Castle Mill stream, one of the many branches of the Thames in Oxford*

8 LEFT, BELOW *The Parish church of St. Peter-in-the-East, now the Library of St. Edmund Hall, seen from the south. It combines Romanesque and Gothic, and demonstrates the sound conservation principle of practical new use*

9 LEFT *The Romanesque chancel of St. Peter-in-the-East, with its robust chain ornament to the vault ribs of c. 1160*

10 *The Romanesque crypt under the chancel of St. Peter-in-the-East. Constructed in the first half of the twelfth century, the crypt is an elaborate pilgrimage or shrine room originally approached by stairs from the nave*

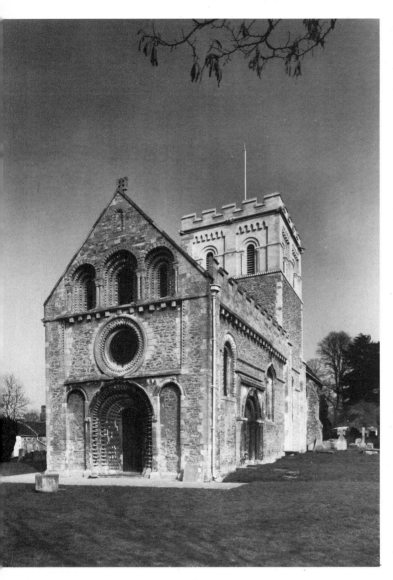

11 The Romanesque village church of St. Mary the Virgin at Iffley, situated on the Thames south of Oxford. Built between 1170–80, it is one of the finest small churches of its period in England. The elaborate beak-heads round the west door and the zig-zag mouldings, are features to be noted. The top storey of the tower was restored in 1976–7

12 ABOVE The parish church of St. Giles stands at the northern edge of the medieval town. There is work of all periods in its building. The fine Early English lancet windows in the north aisle are impressive

13 RIGHT The parish church of St. Mary the Virgin in the High Street, the university church. The fourteenth-century spire is one of the dominant features of the skyline and provides a public viewpoint. The church was rebuilt in the second half of the fifteenth century in a fine Perpendicular Gothic style. The restored late-medieval front of All Souls College is seen to the right

14 *The nave of St. Mary the Virgin looking east to the chancel screen. The beautiful nave was built 1487–1510 and refurnished in 1827. The fittings still reflect the university association, with throne for the Vice-Chancellor at the university sermon, but the main ceremonial moved to the Sheldonian Theatre after 1669*

15 *The chancel of St. Mary the Virgin. Beyond the screen the chancel forms a single tall, aisle-less Perpendicular space of great quality, with good woodwork and monuments*

16 RIGHT *The early eighteenth-century parish church of All Saints, now the library of Lincoln College, still dominates the High Street. Completed in 1708 to a design by Henry Aldrich, Dean of Christ Church, it has the serene quality of its period*

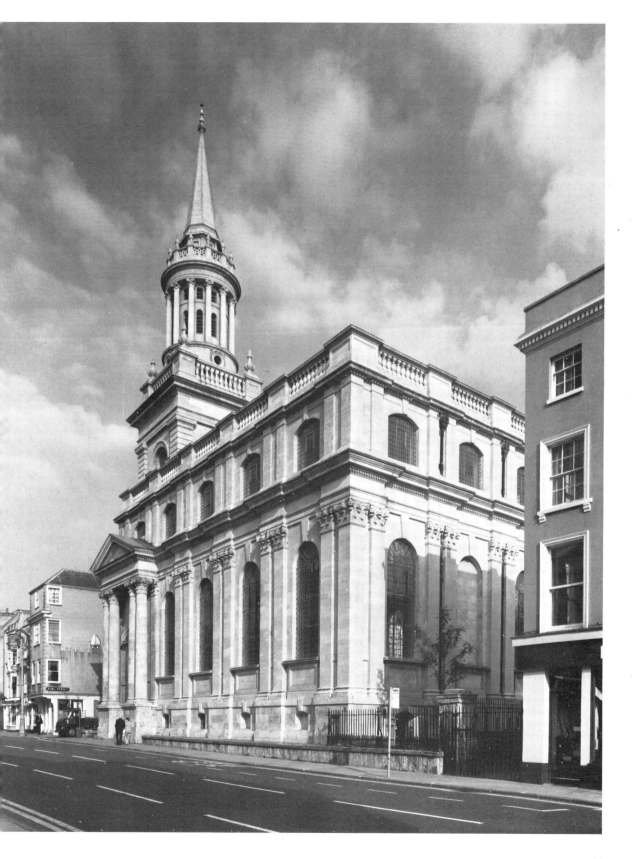

17 *The late Saxon tower of St. Michael at the North Gate confronts the timber-framed 28 Cornmarket Street, the finest surviving late-medieval town house in Oxford, built* c. *1470 and restored 1952*

18 ABOVE RIGHT *The Old Palace: 86 St. Aldàte's. The fine early seventeenth-century town house, now occupied by the Roman Catholic chaplaincy to the University, with its decorative stucco and woodwork*

19 RIGHT *The elaborate plaster ceiling contained within the Old Palace, c. 1630*

20 FAR RIGHT, ABOVE *Merton Street. The medieval and seventeenth-century houses at the west end of the north side. The small building at the centre is Beam Hall (No. 3), built in the late fifteenth century as an academic hall and one of the few survivors of the halls of the medieval University. Beyond is Postmasters Hall (No. 5), where the seventeenth-century antiquary Anthony Wood lived. The houses belong to Merton College*

21 FAR RIGHT *Merton Street. The post-medieval houses at the east end of the north side. No. 15 on the left was described as 'new built' in 1699*

22 LEFT *Holywell Street. The north side at the west end. No. 35, the house with gabled dormers at the centre, is dated 1626 on a window bracket. The house now belongs to Wadham College. The tree indicates the position of the set-back for the music room of 1742*

23 BELOW LEFT *Holywell Street. These eighteenth-century bayed fronts hide many older buildings, and now form part of Manchester College*

24 *Holywell Street. The narrow-fronted houses on the north side at the east end, built in the Manor of Holywell on Merton College land. The seventeenth-century rubble-stone house at the centre, in the Cotswold manner, contrasts with the gabled and plastered framed houses on each side*

25 LEFT, ABOVE *High Street. The south side looking east to the Victorian, King Edward Street. The majority of the houses have flat-fronted, late eighteenth- or early nineteenth-century timber and plaster façades. Those on the right hide seventeenth-century or earlier structures, one with a fine wall painting of* c. *1630*

26 LEFT *St. Giles. The west side looking north, well illustrating the delights of variety in English town buildings. Late eighteenth-century ashlar, much altered late-medieval, narrow mid-nineteenth-century revival, seventeenth-century gables, and so on as far as the eye can see*

27 Beaumont Street. The formal qualities of the late Georgian terrace house, built here after 1824 as part of a new residential quarter by the St. John's College Estates. The equally late Neo-Classical grandeur of the Ashmolean Museum of 1839–45 rises beyond

28 *At the west end of St. Mary's Church, in the former School Street or Radcliffe Street, these gabled seventeenth-century houses owe their detail and present appearance to a restoration by H. W. Moore in the late nineteenth century. They now house the bursary of Brasenose College*

29 BELOW *High Street. These buildings now all form part of Queen's College or St. Edmund Hall. The tall, gabled town house is seventeenth-century, that with the modelled eighteenth-century front was built in 1970, the flat façade next to it in 1976. No. 48 on the right was two seventeenth-century houses, given a flat façade in the eighteenth century, provided with a shopfront in the nineteenth century and repaired and conserved in 1977. The shop at No. 48 was W. R. Morris' cycle and motor-cycle shop between 1901–8*

30 RIGHT *The Martyrs' Memorial, designed by George Gilbert Scott in 1840, and built 1841–3, terminates the south end of St. Giles and recalls the burning in Broad Street of Latimer, Ridley and Cranmer in 1555–6. C. R. Cockerell's superb Taylor Institute of 1839–45 stands behind and forms part of the Ashmolean Museum group*

The Institutional Buildings
of the University

The coat of arms of the University of Oxford as on the vault of the
gate tower to the Schools Quadrangle, *c.* 1620

32 The vaulted interior of the Old Congregation House, attached to St. Mary the Virgin Church. Built in the 1320s, as a result of Bishop Cobham's bequest, this is the oldest building constructed by the University for its own purposes. This vaulted lower room was for meetings, and the first university library was housed in the room above between 1410 and 1490

33 The magnificently vaulted interior of the Schola-Theologica or Divinity School was begun shortly after 1424, but was not completed until 1483 when William Orchard's masterpiece of lierne ribs, bosses and paired dropped pendants was in place. This meeting and teaching room is the most significant interior of the medieval University

34 LEFT, ABOVE The Duke Humfrey Library was built above the Divinity School between 1483 and 1490, to replace that over the Old Congregation House and to house major gifts of books. This room is still the central focus of the Bodleian Library

35 LEFT The wooden ceiling and trusses of Duke Humfrey's Library were wonderfully decorated for Sir Thomas Bodley by 1602. On the panels are painted the arms of the University with Bodley's own arms attached to the cross beams

36 ABOVE The early seventeenth-century Schools Quadrangle now forms the court and entrance to the Bodleian Library and the Divinity School. The Proscholium, with the Arts End of Duke Humfrey's Library over, was built by Bodley between 1610 and 1612. The hard, straight-jacketed, panelled façade well demonstrates the single-minded nature of Oxford's late-Perpendicular Gothic

37 The fine bronze statue of William Herbert, Earl of Pembroke, Chancellor of the University 1617–30, cast by Le Sueur, now stands at the entrance to the Bodleian Library

38 FAR LEFT *The spectacular but clumsily applied scheme of architectural orders on the west face of the tower to the Schools Quadrangle. Sir Thomas Bodley's regeneration of the central library of the University was continued by the rebuilding of the Schools between 1613 and 1620 under the Yorkshire masons John Akroyd and John Bentley. The Schools have been occupied by the Bodleian Library since the nineteenth century*

39 *The Convocation House was added to the west end of the Divinity School in 1634–7 and has excellent oak fittings and panelling. The throne for the chancellor stands at the south end between the facing benches of this 'parliament' chamber*

40 LEFT *The screen of grotesque 'Emperors'' heads which guard the Sheldonian Theatre from Broad Street. Those seen here were replaced in 1972, having themselves replaced earlier ones which had decayed in Victorian times*

41 *The south pedimented façade of the Sheldonian Theatre, designed by Christopher Wren in 1663–4, when he was 31 years of age. The stonework is now crisp Clipsham dating from the major restoration of 1959–60*

42 RIGHT *The Sheldonian Theatre from the east. The cupola is a replacement of 1838. To the left are the Schools and to the right the Clarendon Building*

43 FAR LEFT *The Old Ashmolean Museum was erected between 1679–83 to house the collections of antiquities and rarities made by John Tradescant and Elias Ashmole and given to the University in 1677. It now houses the University's Museum of the History of Science*

44 *The north façade of the Clarendon Building or Printing House, designed by Nicholas Hawksmoor and erected between 1712 and 1715, which completed the University's development facing Broad Street. The Delegates of the Press still meet in the building, but printing had moved to Walton Street by 1830*

45 LEFT *The interior of the meeting room of the Delegates of the University Press in the Clarendon Building*

46 LEFT *The Radcliffe Camera or Library, seen in the early morning from the north quadrangle of All Souls College, with Hawksmoor's hybrid-style cloister screen and ogee cupola set against James Gibbs' classical rotunda and dome, built between 1737 and 1749*

47 ABOVE *The ground-floor reading room of the Radcliffe Camera. When first created, this domed*

and arcaded space functioned as a spacious, open entrance hall to the library above. It was glazed, and converted to library use when the modern north entrance to the Camera was made in 1863

48 *The beautiful Radcliffe Camera staircase, with its heavy wrought-iron balustrade, rises below a fine plasterwork ceiling, to the main reading room*

49 *The main first-floor reading room of the Radcliffe Camera, a vast monumental space below the dome. Rysbrack's statue of the donor, Dr. John Radcliffe, stands over the entrance*

50 BELOW *The early Classical Daubeny Gate to the Botanic Gardens, designed in 1632 by Nicholas Stone. A triumphant Roman entrance to the oldest English Physic Garden*

51 *The superb Radcliffe Observatory on the Woodstock Road. Inspired by the Tower of the Winds at Athens the Observatory was commenced to designs of Henry Keene in 1772 but improved and completed by 1794 under the direction of James Wyatt. It demonstrates how science buildings can be as beautiful as libraries. The panels of decoration lower down, including the series of zodiac signs, are in crisp London artificial Coade stone. The meteorological instruments which for so long disfigured the roof-line of the tower, were removed in 1978. The building is now to become the 'fine rooms' of the new Green Medical College*

52 *The interior of the observing room showing the gallery and fine domed plaster ceiling of the 1780s*

53 *The printing offices in Walton Street, built 1826–30 for the Clarendon Press. The Roman triumphal arch leads to a quadrangle surrounded by workshops, with the former printer's residence at the centre. These fine Classical buildings were designed by Danniel Robertson and completed by Edward Blore*

54 *The Taylor Institute and the University Galleries, the latter now the Ashmolean Museum, 1839–45, at the junction of Beaumont Street and St. Giles. The dramatic façade treatment was by one of England's greatest Neo-classical architects, C. R. Cockerell*

55 The portico forming the main entrance to the Ashmolean Museum

56 The University Museum in Parks Road, designed by Thomas Deane and Benjamin Woodward and built 1855–60. The symmetrical Gothic façade is a reminder that the fine series of Classical buildings erected for the University was at an end. Now beautifully conserved, much of the detailed carving to the façade is seen never to have been completed. The lawn in front, too precious to build on, lies over the two-storey extension of the Radcliffe Science Library of 1976

57 The interior court of the University Museum can come as a surprise with its use of structural cast-iron and glass tiles. While contemporary with the Paxtons' London Crystal Palace, this Victorian Gothic hall did not owe any inspiration to the earlier building and achieves an utterly different result. Between the functional trusses and sitting on clustered iron columns are screens of elaborate naturalistic palm branches. Ruskin, who did not like iron, approved

58 The University Examination Schools are situated at the east end of High Street. The scale is heroic and the style, Elizabethan-Renaissance, displays the skill and historical knowledge of Thomas Jackson. To Jackson belongs the credit of introducing Clipsham stone to Oxford in this vast complex of buildings finished in 1882

59 The interior of the Old Library, formerly the Debating Room, of the Oxford Union Society, hidden off Cornmarket's Frewin Court. It was designed in 1857 by Benjamin Woodward. The paintings above the gallery were done by William Morris and his friends shortly after. Morris later painted the overall leaves of the high ceiling. The remarkable central double fireplaces are served by an underfloor flue

60 The former Indian Institute closes the end of Broad Street, and was designed by Basil Champneys, 1883–96. Its fine interiors now serve the History Faculty libraries

61 The Rhodes Trustees in South Parks Road are established in an over-mannered mixing of Classical forms and vernacular Cotswold massing designed by Sir Herbert Baker in 1929. The interiors are spacious and fine

The Buildings of The Colleges

The medieval seal of the University

All Souls College

Henry Chichele, Archbishop of Canterbury, founded All Souls in 1438, with the support of Henry VI. Its location is a fine one on the High Street at the centre of the medieval city. The buildings make three startling architectural contrasts, once the subtleties of the eighteenth-century design are appreciated. The medieval two-storeyed front quadrangle (1438–43) survives with the chapel and the Old Library. The north quadrangle, with dining hall and the Codrington Library (1716–35), by Nicholas Hawksmoor in his own blend of English Baroque with Gothic, interlocks with the medieval work and externally respects its elevational treatment. The cloister screen and gate (1722–34) to Radcliffe Square make a telling comparison to Hawksmoor's functionally similar screen at Queen's College (1733–6) in his Italian Baroque manner. The warden's house (1706) on High Street, by George Clarke, is by contrast one of the earliest examples of the correct Palladian style in England. All Souls remains a society for Fellows, without undergraduate or graduate members.

62 The fifteenth-century High Street front, with the famous Sycamore tree and Queen's College beyond

*63 The north
quadrangle, with the
Radcliffe Camera at
the left, and Nicholas
Hawksmoor's Gothic
Codrington Library,
begun 1716, on the
right. The reset sundial
is of 1659, by Wren*

*64 Hawksmoor's
towers in the east range
of the north quadrangle
of 1716–48, seen from
the cloister walk.
Triumphant
eighteenth-century
Gothic with double
hung sash windows*

65 The dining-hall
block from the south,
1730–41, by Nicholas
Hawksmoor

67 Hawksmoor's oval
Buttery has graduated
coffering to its ceiling.
A miniature tour-de-
force of enclosure

66 *The sumptuous interior of the dining hall looking east to the screen's passage and gallery. Hawksmoor's ceiling looks as if it is held in tension by constantly rising conversation*

68 The fifteenth-century undercroft under the chapel contains the statues of Henry VI and Archbishop Chichele, removed from the street façade of the gate tower. They are rare survivals of the 1440s

69 The magnificent screen of 1664, remodelled 1716, placed across the medieval chapel of 1442

70 RIGHT The north recess in the Codrington Library, with bookcases and a marble statue of Christopher Codrington by Henry Cheere, 1734

71 FAR RIGHT The interior of the ground-floor Codrington Library, begun by Hawksmoor and completed by 1750 after further advice from James Gibbs. It is the longest library room in Oxford and it is curious that this English Baroque interior has a Gothic exterior

Balliol College

Balliol College, founded by John of Balliol of County Durham in the 1260s on a site in the parish of St. Mary Magdalen just north of the walled city, has undemonstrative late-medieval buildings. Architecturally, the eye is more aware of Alfred Waterhouse's tall chambers (1867) set over Broad Street and his dining hall (1876) set in the beautiful garden quadrangle towards St. Giles. Waterhouse's buildings vie with William Butterfield's chapel (1856), and contrast with the suitably aggressive modern blocks flanking the dining hall in the garden quadrangle

72 The dramatic confrontations of the front quadrangle. The fifteenth-century library, left, adjoins William Butterfield's chapel of 1856 and Alfred Waterhouse's chambers of 1867, right

73 RIGHT *The fifteenth-century dining hall and library in the front quadrangle. The location and rhythm of the windows make clear the original functions*

74 Interior of the fifteenth-century first-floor library as remodelled and refurnished by James Wyatt in 1792–4

75 *The west side of the fifteenth-century hall, now converted as the modern library*

76 *The Victorian dining hall in the garden quadrangle. The hall is by Alfred Waterhouse, 1876, its companions by Geoffrey Beard, 1965–8*

Brasenose College

Brasenose was founded in 1509 by Sir
Richard Sutton and William Smith,
Bishop of Lincoln, on land at the centre
of the medieval city, adjoining the
University's Schools. It has grown to
form three quadrangles and its gate
tower now confronts the bulk of the
Radcliffe Camera at close quarters. The
chapel quadrangle, which the chapel
shares with the kitchen and first-floor
library, is mid-seventeenth-century and
now leads to Thomas Jackson's large
new quadrangle (completed between
1886–1909). Tucked away behind this on
a virtually non-existent site is a complex
piece of college infill of the 1960s, best
seen from All Saints' churchyard.

*77 The spectacular view to the gate tower set
against the Radcliffe Camera from the old
quadrangle. The ranges of rooms here were built
1509–16 and were raised with the gabled dormer
windows in 1604–36. The oriel window indicates
the dining hall to the right*

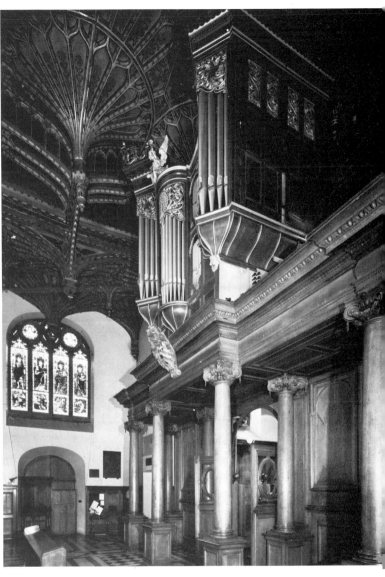

78 LEFT *The interior of the dining hall, with its rich panelling of 1684 and coved plaster ceiling inserted 1754*

79 *The first-floor library over the originally open cloister facing the second quadrangle was begun in 1664 in Oxford's blend of Classical and Gothic*

80 *The fine interior of the library, as remodelled and ceiled in 1780 by James Wyatt*

81 *The interior of the chapel seen from the antechapel, with Thomas Jackson's screen of 1892 and the remarkable plaster fan vault of 1659 above by John Jackson*

82 *The excellent High Street façade of new quadrangle built from Thomas Jackson's design between 1886–1909 and cleaned in 1978. Beyond can be seen a few remaining town houses, once the dominant feature of the High here*

Christ Church

Thomas Wolsey, Cardinal and statesman, Bishop of Lincoln and Archbishop of York, founded Cardinal College in 1525 on the site occupied by the buildings of the dissolved Augustinian Priory of St. Frideswide within the city-wall at South Gate. The college was refounded by the King in 1532, after Wolsey's fall, as King Henry VIII College; and in 1546 Henry created Christ Church as a union of College and Cathedral Church for the Diocese of Oxford. The College and Cathedral Church of Christ in Oxford is thus a unique foundation, with the Dean presiding over the governing body of the college.

From the monastic period, the church and extensive remains of claustral buildings survive. Wolsey's unfinished Great Quadrangle, the most spacious at Oxford, is late-medieval in design and concept and set out to follow the precedent, established at Magdalen, of uniting cloister into quad. Peckwater Quadrangle, which occupies the site of the dissolved Canterbury College, is one of the most formal of Oxford's eighteenth-century spaces.

Given its expansive site, Christ Church is divided into a surprising number of related, but not necessarily visually related, spaces and gardens. Blue Boar Quadrangle and the below-ground Picture Gallery have added to this complexity in the 1960s.

83 The Great Gate, 1526, and Tom Tower, 1681, from Pembroke Square

RADCLIFFE
CAMERA

84 LEFT *The St. Aldate's façade of Christ Church. The elaborated ogee-capped towers of the gate of Wolsey's College contrast with the plainer side ranges, while above looms Christopher Wren's sympathetic bell-tower*

85 *The unfinished Great Quadrangle of Christ Church. The two-storey ranges represent Wolsey's scheme. The corner shadow hides the hall entrance and staircase under Thomas Bodley's belfry tower of 1879. The modest entrances below the spire giving access to the Cathedral are also of this date*

86 ABOVE *A high-level view, from Bodley's belfry, of the Early-English Gothic spire of the mid-thirteenth century, rising above the Romanesque tower of the Cathedral*

87 *The nave, crossing and choir of the Cathedral Church of Christ built for the Augustine canons of the Priory of St. Fridswide. The Romanesque arcades of 1180–1210 are gathered together in the choir by the lierne vault raised in the late fifteenth century. The majority of the fittings belong to the restoration in the 1870s by Scott*

88 The choir vault: one of the most magnificent vaults in England. While undocumented, its close relationship to William Orchard's vault in the University's Divinity School is undoubted, and it must belong to the closing years of the fifteenth century. The great spanning arches which disappear into the vault carry a complexity of ribs, bosses and plumeting pendants

89 The superb stained glass in the east window of the lady chapel by William Morris and Edward Burne-Jones of 1872–3

90 The dining-hall stair compartment belongs to Wolsey's work, but was not given its Perpendicular fan vault until the middle years of the seventeenth century. The present stone stairs were contrived by James Wyatt in 1801–4

91 The dining-hall, the largest of Medieval Oxford, spanned by hammer-beam trusses with pendants. Built, under Cardinal Wolsey's direction between 1525–9, for his Cardinal College

92 A precious survival is the fragment of roof painted with armorial panels, originally decorating the library built by Otho Nicholson for Christ Church, 1610–12. The library, now divided into residential sets, was created out of the late fifteenth-century refectory of St. Fridewide's Priory.

93 RIGHT Peckwater Quadrangle. This formal Palladian three-sided range of residential sets was designed by Henry Aldrich, Dean of Christ Church, and built by Townsend between 1706–11

94 The monumental north façade to Peckwater Quadrangle of the eighteenth-century library of Christ Church is the grandest Italian Renaissance work in Oxford. Built between 1717 and 1738 to a design by George Clarke, it is also a fine example of contemporary restoration, being totally and very successfully refaced in Portland and Clipsham stones between 1960 and 1962. The ground floor, originally intended as an open arcade, was closed in 1764

95 *The interior of the first-floor library, fitted up and decorated between 1752 and 1763 with superb joinery, the gallery carried on an Ionic order. The attractive Rococo plasterwork to the ceiling is by Thomas Roberts*

96 *The Canterbury Gateway with a Doric order by James Wyatt, 1773–78, forms a refined back entrance to Christ Church from Oriel Square and Merton street*

Corpus Christi College

Richard Foxe, statesman and Bishop of Winchester, founded Corpus Christi College in 1517. The college occupies a small site in comparison with Christ Church and Merton, its neighbours along the southern city-wall. The founder's buildings comprised a single, small, two-storeyed quadrangle with gate tower, dining hall, chapel and library carefully integrated into the four ranges with the residential sets. Expansion in the eighteenth century followed the normal Oxford pattern, with the erection of a new quad, formed by a Fellows' Building that faces over a superbly sited garden overlooking the city-wall. More recent residential sets have had to be located across Merton Street along Magpie Lane.

97 The recently paved front quadrangle looking to the gate tower, with the exquisitely restored sundial of 1581, with its perpetual calendar first added in 1666

98 LEFT *The late sixteenth-century plaster ceiling in the room over the gate tower, provided for the early Presidents of the College*

99 *The early eighteenth-century arcade in the cloister quadrangle*

100 ABOVE *The interior of the chapel, built in the foundation years and given its present fittings in 1676–7. The fine screen to the antechapel may be a little later*

101 *The interior of the first-floor library, complete by 1517, preserves the original arrangement of benches between lectern-desks, but the latter were raised with shelves in the seventeenth century. The roof was ceiled in 1843*

102 The Fellows' Building of 1706–12, by Henry Aldrich, from the garden just within the southern city-wall

Exeter College

Walter de Stapledon, statesman and Bishop of Exeter, founded Stapledon Hall in 1314. Exeter achieved full college status in 1566 when Sir William Petre re-endowed the foundation. The site was a constrained and urban one, in the centre of the city, originally tight up against the city-wall. The buildings comprised a single quadrangle with little external display until the nineteenth century. The erection of the chapel changed that. The beautiful and hidden Fellows' Garden contains the nineteenth-century library and forms a setting for the University's Convocation House and the Divinity School. The garden is sheltered by high walls from Brasenose Lane and Radcliffe Square.

103 The main quadrangle is overawed by George Gilbert Scott's massive chapel of 1856–9, with its vigorously modelled façade and tall lead flèche. The gate tower to the left was rebuilt in a Classical style in 1701, but the elevations were made Gothic again in 1833

104 The high vaulted interior of the chapel, with fittings by Bodley, 1884 is a rich example of High Victorian Gothic, medieval French in inspiration

105 The chapel contains a wonderful treasure in the tapestry, commissioned for the building and made by William Morris to the design of Edward Burne-Jones in 1890, illustrating the adoration of the Magi

106 RIGHT The interior of the dining hall, 1618, well shows how medieval in appearance early seventeenth-century Oxford architecture appears. However, the trusses are more interested in being decorative than in expressing their structural design

107 George Gilbert Scott's attractive small library, 1856, stands in the hidden Fellows' Garden, adjoining the University's Convocation House

Hertford College

Hertford College was refounded in 1874 by Thomas Baring, from the less vigorous earlier combinations of Magdalen Hall with Hart Hall and Hertford College, which were medieval in origins. The buildings of Hertford naturally reflect this slow evolution to its present size. The diminutive hall of Hart Hall and the old chapel (now library) contrast with Thomas Jackson's rebuilding and expansion which jumped over New College Lane in the first half of the twentieth century. The 1970s have seen the sensitive addition of a third quad towards Holywell Street.

108 The front quadrangle, with Thomas Jackson's entrance block with the remarkable staircase leading to the dining hall above, 1887. An architectural reference to the Ile de France is here evident

109 The Hertford Bridge over New College Lane, with Thomas Jackson again playing architectural travel games inappropriate to the character of Oxford, 1913

110 BELOW Jackson's dining hall, of 1887, a more restrained, flat-ceilinged room appropriate to its function

111 FAR RIGHT The interior of the Hertford chapel is another matter. One of the least-known interiors of drama in Oxford, and Thomas Jackson at his best. The historian's borrowing here is skilfully used. The east window is better known as a façade seen from Queen's Lane

Jesus College

Dr. Hugh Price founded Jesus College in 1571 with the support of Queen Elizabeth I. The college occupies a typical, central urban site within the walled city behind the busy Cornmarket Street. The two main quadrangles hug the site boundaries with tall ranges and the lack of space has forced modern expansion to adopt ingenious solutions towards Cornmarket.

112 First quadrangle is partly founder's work and partly of 1617–30. The chapel to the left belongs to this latter phase as does the upper storey of the range to the right. Exeter's flèche across Turl Street competes with the gate tower

113 RIGHT The interior of the chapel, a basically seventeenth-century structure, illustrates well the modifications of the Victorians (in this case George Edmund Street in 1864). The screen, preserved from the late seventeenth century, remains

114 The interior of the dining hall of 1617, with warm, oak panelling. The plasterwork and ceiling of the roof trusses dates to 1741

115 The inner quadrangle, built between 1640 and 1713, displays a startling single-mindedness in the elevational treatment of its three storeys, with its Jacobean-shaped decorative gables jostling for space. Only the importance of the Classical door, in the Gothic wall, indicates the presence of the library within

116 *The interior of the library, completed 1679 but fitted with the bookcases and seating from the earlier library of 1626*

117 *A fine seventeenth-century interior in the Principal's lodgings*

Keble College

Keble College, which received its charter in 1868, was founded as a result of the subscriptions received from admirers of the work and life of the Rev. John Keble, and to reinforce the 'Oxford Movement' in the life of the Anglican Church. The College opened in 1870 and its buildings were designed by William Butterfield. The uncompromising brick-and-stone High-Victorian architecture has long been controversial, but its strong individual character should only give pleasure

today. The expansion of Keble in the late twentieth century is equally dramatic with its high brick-and-glass façades. Keble has a suburban setting and links the historic City to the North Oxford Victorian suburb.

118 The summit for the Tractarians and their High-Victorian Gothic architecture in Oxford. The 'constructional polychromy' of William Butterfield's brick and stone has recently been overhauled. The chapel was consecrated in 1876, and is on a vast scale, but then so is the quadrangle

119 FAR LEFT *A detail of the elaborate decoration and structural colour of a bay of the chapel by the pulpit. The mosaic pictures are by A. Gibbs*

120 *The interior of the enormous dining hall*

121 *A characteristic fire-place, to a design by William Butterfield in the dining hall. The monogram is for John Keble*

Lincoln College

The College of the Blessed Mary and All Saints, Lincoln, in the University of Oxford, was founded by Richard Fleming, Bishop of Lincoln in 1427. Like its neighbours, Exeter and Jesus, it is located on a small urban site at the centre of the walled city. Its buildings, which gradually expanded southwards, also hug its street frontages tightly. The front quadrangle retains its fifteenth-century appearance, with the ranges remaining two storeys in height. The College now uses the former parish church of All Saints as its library.

122 The Turl Street front with the gate tower built in 1437, but refaced in 1824. The tall chimney stacks remind one of the residential use of the ranges

123 RIGHT The two-storeyed, fifteenth-century front quadrangle with entrance tower, left and north range, right. This originally contained the chapel, later converted to a library, and now a common room on the first floor, entered through the large doorway

124 The dining hall of 1436, with panelling of 1701 and side chimney-piece by Jackson 1891. The fine arched-braced roof was at one stage ceiled and was happily re-exposed in the late nineteenth century

125 *The south side of the late-Gothic chapel of 1629–31, from the Rector's garden*

126 RIGHT *A detail of the east window of the chapel made by Bernard van Linge in 1631. Jonah spewed onto dry land by the great fish, and Elisha watching Elijah carried to heaven*

127 FAR RIGHT *The bench-end figure of St. Mark gives an indication of the quality of the seventeenth-century woodwork in the chapel*

128 The upper reading room in Henry Aldrich's Church of All Saints, 1708, remodelled as the Lincoln College Library by Robert Potter in 1975. This major work of conservation involved the raising of the floor level, by the height of the steps, and the excavation of two new rooms below. The fine new fittings incorporate some earlier carved work

Magdalen College

The College of the St. Mary Magdalen was founded by William of Waynflete, Bishop of Winchester in 1458 shortly after he became Lord Chancellor. In its size, status and endowment Waynflete emulated Wykeham's New College. The chosen site was that occupied by the suppressed Hospital of St. John, just outside the walled city on the east, by the road-crossing of the river Cherwell towards London.

The buildings had been set out by 1473, to a carefully planned layout by the master mason William Orchard, who integrated the cloister within the great quadrangle, an important rearrangement of the New College plan. The architecture is the national Perpendicular Gothic of the Royal Court. Several buildings of the Hospital of St. John were retained and the foundation phase of the buildings was completed by the construction of the bell-tower in 1492–1509. The isolated Classical New Building of 1733 represents the built fragment of a grandiose rebuilding plan. Expansion in the late nineteenth and twentieth centuries has been towards Longwall, creating spacious linked quadrangles. The whole environment of Magdalen is spacious, allowing the retention of a walled deer park, and the creation of water walks along the Cherwell, in strong contrast to the urban city-centre colleges.

129 The College from the High Street, before the wholesale restoration of its fabric in recent years. The two-storey wing along the street contains the remains of the chapel of the Hospital of St. John

130 FAR LEFT The great bell-tower of Magdalen, one of the greatest towers of medieval England, finished in 1509 by master mason William Raynold, seen before the present restoration. Magdalen Bridge, of 1772–7 and widened in 1882, spans a branch of the river Cherwell in the foreground

131 The great cloistered quadrangle 1470–90, with dining hall and chapel to the left and founder's tower and library to the right. Master mason, William Orchard

132 The cloister walk, at the original entrance under the vaulted founder's tower. The lierne vault and fine bosses contrast with the simple beamed corridor beyond

133 LEFT *The interior of the dining hall, completed by 1490, with the present roof restored in 1902 by Thomas Bodley. The fine linen-fold panelling is of the early sixteenth century*

134 ABOVE *A detail of the carved centrepiece in the high table panelling dated 1541, illustrating the life of St. Mary Magdalen and celebrating Henry VIII*

135 RIGHT *The spacious interior of the antechapel completed by 1480, with its soaring Perpendicular piers. The organ screen to the chapel belongs to Lewis Cottingham's major restoration of 1830–2. The fine and unusual sepia glass is of 1632, by Richard Greenbury*

136 *A detail of the monument of Richard Patten, c. 1450, father of William of Waynflete, brought to Oxford from Wainfleet, Lincolnshire, in the nineteenth century*

137 *The fifteenth-century quadrangle and the New Building of 1733 by George Clarke seen from the top of the bell-tower. The Cherwell Valley spreads northwards beyond, towards Elsfield.*

Merton College

Walter de Merton, Lord Chancellor and Bishop of Rochester, had founded his College by 1264. In Oxford, from 1266 onwards, land for building was purchased adjoining the parish church of St. John the Baptist, just within the south-east corner of the walled city. The present buildings include the oldest college buildings in Oxford, with Mob Quad the first evolved quadrangle. The loose layout of the earlier quadrangles at Merton lacks the formal planning of later work. The medieval chapel is the finest Gothic church in the city after St. Mary the Virgin, and retained its parish status until 1891. The historic accident of its uncompleted plan form, comprising of chancel, tower and transepts, lead to the regular use of the chancel and antechapel plan form in other Oxford colleges. The Fellows' Quadrangle of 1610 is the first built of three storeys in the University, and the adjoining Fellows' Garden has unrivalled views over the southern meadows from the city-wall-top walk.

138 The dramatic townscape of Merton Street with the dining hall of Corpus Christi College on the right, Oriel College Chapel to the left and the former Church of St. John, now Merton College Chapel, with its tower of 1448–51 designed by Robert Jannyns

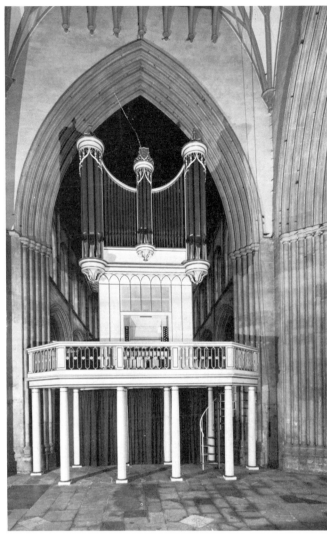

139 LEFT The tower of the chapel from the fourteenth-century Mob Quadrangle, with a range of the first-floor library of 1373–8 on the left. The unique dormers were added in 1597–8, and the residential north range of 1335 is in rubble-stone

140 The crossing arches of 1300–1335 under the tower of the chapel. The crossing and transepts form an antechapel without a nave. The choir of 1290–7 to the right, through Wren's screen of 1671, contains important medieval stained glass

141 The crossing arch of the projected nave, filled by Robert Potter's organ case and gallery of 1968 and the surprising trompe l'oeil *painting of the nave. It hides the west window*

142 *A detail of a bay in the east wing of the library, refitted in 1623, retaining elements of the fourteenth-century arrangements. Note that this bay also retains the facilities for chaining the books, a practice that did not generally die out in Oxford libraries until the end of the eighteenth century*

143 *The three-storey Fellows' Quadrangle, one of the first in Oxford, with its frontispiece of a tower of architectural orders. Under Warden Savile, John Akroyd and John Bentley of Halifax built the masonry in 1609–10. The well-preserved Headington stonework has recently been carefully cleaned and the frontispiece restored*

144 The Tudor royal coat of arms on the vault of the Fitzjames Gateway of c. 1500, leading to the Fellows' Quadrangle

145 The spectacular oak roof of the Aula Custodis, now the middle common room, in the Merton Street range, was built as the hall of the warden's private house in 1299. The construction of the trusses is unusual, with its sturdy, decorated queen-posts supporting a crown-post

146 The College seen from Merton Field with the city-wall forming a firm boundary between town and country almost at the centre of Oxford. Mob Quad and the library are hidden behind the fine trees

147 RIGHT *New College. The gate tower and lodge, 1380–6, from New College Lane a chasm of blackened, blank walls between the cloister of 1400 and Warden's Barn, and a total contrast to the spacious quadrangle within, with its lawn*

New College

The founding in 1379 of St. Mary College of Winchester in Oxford, or New College, by William of Wykeham, Bishop of Winchester and twice Lord Chancellor, marked a significant advance in the evolution of the college system in Oxford. Wykeham's long-considered educational concept involved much more than the necessary purchase of land, site clearance, closure or diversion of streets, and the undertaking of the maintenance of a long stretch of city-wall. His vision, spelt out in the college statutes, entailed the provision of a group of buildings housing 70 people (with the students forming part of the same body as the senior Fellows and tutors) and linked to Wykeham School at Winchester. The layout of the buildings, erected between 1380 and 1400, based on a formal quadrangle and separate cloister, is precisely regular, with elevations in the early Perpendicular style favoured by the Royal Court.

While the entrance from New College Lane is the most blankly walled in Oxford, the creation of gardens within the inner angle of the city-wall beyond the main buildings has given New College a remarkably spacious green setting, at the heart of the once densely populated medieval City. The medieval buildings are an impressive survival, even if account has to be taken of the additional storey added to the residential ranges in the seventeenth century and the expansion eastwards towards the gardens. The greater nineteenth-century expansion was made north of the city-wall along Holywell Street. It is from the north, over the site of the city ditch, that William Wynford's architectural design is best appreciated, with the chapel, dining hall and kitchen in line, seen over the bastioned city-wall, with the bell-tower punctuating the view.

148 *The serene cloister, finished by 1400, shuts off the wide west front of the antechapel, complete by 1386. The bell-tower, 1396–1405, stands on the town wall and is constructed in fine-quality Headington stone*

149 FAR RIGHT *The interior of the chapel, 1380–6, by William Wynford master mason, with the spectacular reredos. The roof, reredos and stalls woodwork belong to the restorations of 1877–92, but follow the medieval arrangements and the misericords have been preserved*

150 RIGHT *The Perpendicular tracery of the west window, with the strange painted glass designed by Sir Joshua Reynolds and made by Thomas Jarvis in 1778–85. The upper light illustrates the Nativity and the lower the Seven Virtues*

151 *The open-sided
Garden Quadrangle is
closed by a wrought-iron
screen, with a gate
made by Thomas
Robinson in 1711*

152 *The New College
garden sits within the
medieval city-wall, here
screened by a wide
herbaceous border, and
comprises fine lawns
and an overgrown
mound*

Oriel College

The House of the Blessed Mary the Virgin in Oxford, or Oriel College, was founded in 1326 by the Rector of St. Mary the Virgin church, Adam de Broome, with the support of Edward II. However, no medieval buildings survive on the tight urban site south of the High Street, in the centre of the walled city. The front quadrangle belongs to the early seventeenth-century rebuilding, reflecting the new work at Wadham, and is similarly late-Gothic in design, but with the addition of gables. The eighteenth-century expansion in the back quadrangle was at first built in the same conservative Gothic, but is now dominated by the massive Neo-classical library. St. Mary Hall, with origins in the fourteenth century, was absorbed by Oriel in 1902. Its irregular buildings now form the northern quadrangle of the College behind the Rhodes Building on High Street.

153 The front quadrangle of Oriel College, built 1620–42, seen from high over Oriel Square, with the gate tower right. The crowded rows of Jacobean-shaped gables are dominated at this level by the tower of Merton Chapel beyond

154 LEFT The interior of the dining hall, 1637–42, with its heavy hammer-beam roof

155 ABOVE The interior of the chapel, with good woodwork of 1642

156 The library, contained within a fine Neo-classical block of 1788–9 by James Wyatt, is on the first floor, with common rooms below

157 The interior of James Wyatt's Library. Here the books have completely retreated to high wall-cases. The necessary gallery continues round an apse screened by giant Corinthian columns

158 St. Mary Quadrangle of Oriel contains the buildings of St. Mary Hall. As a result of its constricted site, St. Mary Hall built its dining hall and chapel one over the other in a single block in 1639–40. The chapel is now part of the Oriel library. To the left, residential sets in a timber-framed eighteenth-century block

Pembroke College

Thomas Tesdall and Richard Wightwick founded Pembroke College in 1624 as a direct continuation of the medieval Broadgates Hall. The site, always a narrow one, lies along the southern city-wall opposite Christ Church. The two-storey, seventeenth-century main quadrangle and the chapel are placed high above the city-wall. The Victorian expansion contrives to appear remarkably spacious, however, with its precious lawn. The recent expansion over Beef Lane incorporates the historic houses on the south side of Pembroke Street.

159 The chapel quadrangle looking to the seventeenth-century quadrangle, which incorporates the medieval Broadgates Hall, with the chapel, right, built high over the city-wall

160 The interior of the impressive, Victorian dining hall of 1846 by Charles Haywood

161 The interior of the chapel, built by William Townsend 1728–32, still retains much of its original woodwork, plasterwork and reredos. Visually, these are submerged under C. E. Kempe's redecoration of 1884, a rich Neo-renaissance scheme which includes the stained glass and figures standing under canopies

The Radcliffe Camera and Schools Quadrangle seen from Catte Street in Radcliffe Square

The front quadrangle of Oriel College with the approach to the dining hall

The interior of the Sheldonian Theatre, 1669

The interior of Trinity College chapel, 1694

The Tower of Five Orders in the Bodleian Quadrangle

The interior of the Union Library

The chapel of Exeter College

A window in the chapel
of Wadham College

The Queen's College

Robert de Eglesfield, chaplain to Queen Philippa wife of Edward III, founded the Queen's College in 1341. The medieval buildings all perished in the magnificent reconstruction of the College, begun in 1674 and not completed until 1760, which brought Queen's to its significant position on the north curve of the High Street. The sources for the design of its buildings are complex and are associated with the architects Wren, Aldrich, Hawksmoor, Clarke and the mason-contractor Townsend. As a group, the College contains the most important monumental English Baroque buildings in Oxford, with two fine quadrangles separated by dining hall and chapel in line. The series of enclosed gardens behind the small historic houses in the High towards All Souls are memorable for their complexity and views.

162 The monumental Baroque façade of Queen's on the High Street, 1709–36. An open quadrangle closed by a cloister screen, as at Hawksmoor's All Souls. The drama of the design is enhanced by the historic town houses to each side

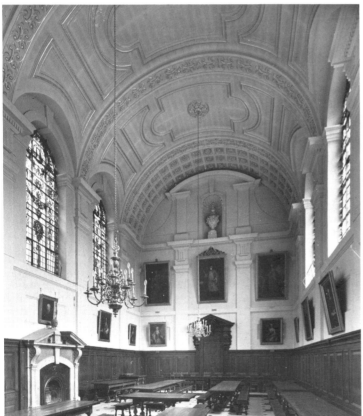

163 FAR LEFT *The Baroque gate by Hawksmoor with its domed cupola finished in 1736*

164 *The front quadrangle is monumental English Baroque and quite different from anything else in Oxford. Residential sets occupy the ranges over the arcades. The dining hall and chapel, separated by a passage, link the centre below the distinctive tower and pedimented centrepiece*

165 *The interior of the dining hall, 1714, probably by Nicholas Hawksmoor or perhaps George Clarke or William Townsend, and totally English Baroque*

166 LEFT The interior of the chapel, 1714, with
its apsed end, fine stalls, excellent plasterwork and
ceiling painting by Thornhill. The glass is of
interest. The east window is by Joshua Price,
1717, but eight other windows contain fine, re-set
glass made by Abraham van Linge in 1634 for the
earlier chapel

167 The North quadrangle is closed on the west by
the library (1692–5). This, the first of the great
show-piece library rooms of Oxford, was perhaps
designed by Henry Aldrich. The ground-floor
arcade was open until 1841

168 FAR LEFT *The impressive first-floor room is also the most attractive interior of the libraries, principally because of its plasterwork decoration. The primary scheme was completed in 1695 by James Hands and to it Thomas Roberts added Rococo work in 1756. Unlike in the later show-room libraries, the fine bookcases do not line the walls, but form traditional stalls with reading-desks*

169 *A detail of the entrance doorcase, with its segmental pediment carrying figures of Arts and Science below the arms of Provost Holton held in a crowd of cherubs*

170 *A detail of the carved cupboard doors by Thomas Minn*

St. Edmund Hall

The college owes its origin to the hall founded in the thirteenth century, and its name enshrines the fact that St. Edmund Hall was the last of the independent academic-halls to achieve full college status in 1957. The main quadrangle is an attractive group of sixteenth- and seventeenth-century buildings which surprisingly adjoin the extensive twentieth-century high-rise block over the new dining hall. The contrast is perhaps the most abrupt in Oxford and not without its pleasure.

The recent conversion of the former parish church of St. Peter-in-the-East into the college library is very successful and brings the churchyard within the college precinct.

171 The old quadrangle is one of the smallest and most attractive in Oxford, and has retained its sixteenth- and seventeenth-century appearance. The early Classical façade (1675–84) is that shared by the library and chapel and retains its cross-casement windows

172 The interior of the small, Old Library contrived in the first-floor room over the antechapel, with its original, but enlarged, gallery arrangement of 1675–84

173 The interior of the new library formed in the nave and north aisle of St. Peter-in-the-East in the early 1970s

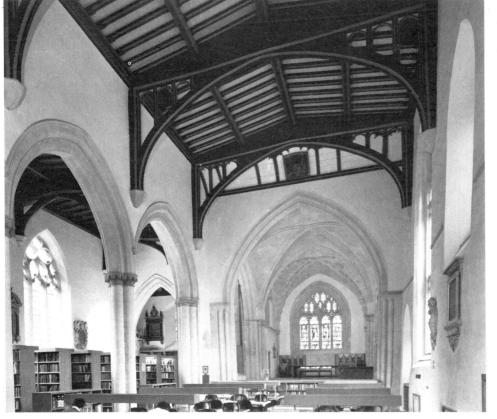

St. John's College

Sir Thomas White founded the College of St. John the Baptist in 1555, using the site and extant buildings of the dissolved Cistercian College of St. Bernard, situated in the spacious northern medieval suburbs of St. Giles. The front quadrangle, with dining hall and chapel, belongs to the pre-Reformation phase. The two first-floor libraries are in ranges of the Canterbury Quadrangle, with its Italian arcades. The north quadrangle replaced town houses in the nineteenth century and leads to the extensive Sir Thomas White Building, completed in 1976. The fine gardens are among the most extensive in Oxford, as befits a college situated on the edge of the medieval City.

174 The fifteenth-century façade and gate tower seen from the forecourt on St. Giles, built for the monastic St. Bernard's College

175 The front *Quadrangle*, *two-storeyed*, *fifteenth-century*, *with the gate tower on the left and the dining hall and chapel on the right*

176 *The interior of the Baylie chapel of 1662, with fine monuments and a plaster fanvault*

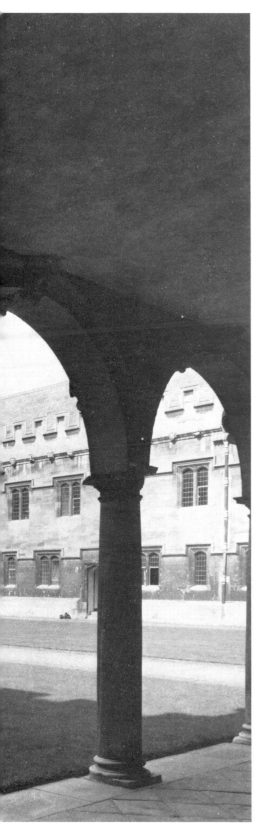

177 LEFT *The early seventeenth-century Canterbury Quadrangle is one of the finest and strangest at Oxford. Essentially late-Perpendicular Gothic, its fundamental character is derived from the Classical centrepieces and arcades. The design (1631–6) may be by Adam Browne, with the client, in the person of Archbishop William Laud, being the dominant factor. The bronze statue of Queen Henrietta Maria is by Le Sueur*

178 The interior of the dining hall, a complete contrast to its sixteenth-century exterior, with a plaster ceiling of 1730 inspired by Queen's. The chimneypiece by William Townsend is also of this date

179 FAR LEFT *A detail of the eastern
centrepiece, with a Le Sueur bronze of Charles I
placed onto the Gothic wall of Laud's Library*

*180 The Laudian Library and Canterbury
Quadrangle seen from the spacious lawns east of the
college buildings. The large projecting oriel window
on the left marks the end of the Old Library. The
elevation also makes a telling contrast to the
arcaded quadrangle within*

*181 The interior of the first-floor Old Library,
1596–1601, situated in the south range of
Canterbury Quadrangle. The bookcases and
reading-desks are contemporary, but the former
were later raised in height. The roof is ceiled at the
collar beam (the omission of the tie-beam has
necessitated later iron tie-rods)*

Trinity College

The College of the Holy and Undivided Trinity, founded by Sir Thomas Pope in 1555, occupies the site and buildings of the suppressed Benedictine Durham College. With St. John's, Trinity shares the once open lands north of the medieval City, east of St. Giles. The situation of its older buildings well back from Broad Street is uncharacteristic of Oxford. The restored town houses on Broad Street, however, are a reminder that the lawns replace the plots of town houses which were gradually incorporated into the college site and finally developed under Thomas Jackson in the late nineteenth century, and by others more recently. The Classical late seventeenth-century chapel and gate tower mark the change to the tight layout of the medieval buildings, with dining hall facing first-floor library. Beyond, the three-sided Garden Quadrangle opens to the fine gardens.

182 *The older college buildings lie well set back from Broad Street. The gate tower and chapel (1691–4) were perhaps designed by Henry Aldrich*

183 *The interior of the chapel is a wonderfully complete piece, oak and juniper wood, carved lime wood, plasterwork and paintings: one of the finest rooms of its time in England. A detail of the carved work of the reredos showing the quality of the craftsmanship*

184 *Durham Quadrangle beyond the chapel recalls the origin of the college as the monastic Durham College. The east range, right, built in 1417–21, contains the first-floor library and, below, rooms with simple, wood ceilings with painted decoration. The left range is of 1728*

185 *These simple seventeenth-century houses, which once separated Trinity from Broad Street, are now incorporated within the College as porter's lodge and residential sets. They are a precious foil to the grander buildings of Broad Street*

186 *The garden quadrangle opens onto the wide Trinity lawns that parallel St. John's Gardens. The wrought-iron screen and gate is a college memorial to those lost in the 1939–45 War*

University College

University College, as its name suggests, is one of the oldest foundations of the University and owes its origins to the bequest of William of Durham in 1249. Formal statutes were granted in 1280. It occupies a central position in the City on the south side of the High Street and, typically, has expanded at the expense of town houses. The front quadrangle, with chapel and dining hall in line and library behind, belongs to a major rebuilding campaign of the early years of the seventeenth century. The architectural style is late-Gothic, with rows of Jacobean shaped gables. The Radcliffe Quadrangle, added along the High Street in 1717–19, continues this conservative architectural style. Nineteenth- and twentieth-century expansion has been possible behind preserved town houses, and fine gardens remain hidden in the area towards the Merton Real Tennis Court on the south.

187 FAR LEFT *The front quadrangle 1634–77, looking towards the gate tower with statue of James II. The three-storeyed elevations of the residential sets are finished with tight regiments of fashionable Jacobean-shaped gables*

188 The south range of the front quadrangle has a Gothic centrepiece with oriels of 1802 and contains the chapel, left, and dining hall, right, set end to end with the kitchen and library behind

189 The interior of the chapel, consecrated in 1666. Its completion was delayed by the Civil War, as the particularly fine series of windows by Abraham van Linge date to 1641. The fine woodwork is of the 1660s and the Corinthian screen of 1694. A disastrous remodelling by Scott in 1862 altered the roof and added unsuitable glass in the east window

190 BELOW *A detail of a van Linge window in the chapel, 1641, illustrating Adam and Eve after the fall; Abraham visited by the Angels; and farming activity in a landscape*

191 The gate tower in the Radcliffe Quadrangle, 1717–19, with the statue of Dr. John Radcliffe, benefactor. The elevational treatment follows that in the front quadrangle and therefore displays a quite remarkable conservatism, but the design was requested by Dr. Radcliffe to be answerable to the old

192 FAR LEFT *The entrance under the Radcliffe gate tower is fan-vaulted, which displays an even more remarkable late-Perpendicular Gothic survival*

193 Equally surprising to find in a college is the memorial to the poet Percy Bysshe Shelley (1792–1822). Strange to recall, he was 'sent down' in 1811. The memorial, set up in 1893, is by E. Onslow Ford and is strikingly set below a dome by Basil Champneys

Wadham College

Nicholas and Dorothy Wadham founded Wadham College in 1610 in the green fields north of the walled city, on the site of the Augustinian friary. The open site allowed a formal symmetrical plan to be adopted, very much in the traditional New College manner, but designed in Oxford's late-Gothic style, enlivened with Classical features. The quadrangle is three-storeyed, and with the contemporary Fellows' Quadrangle at Merton, is of the first with this important development. The buildings have superb gardens on the north, situated just within the seventeenth-century Civil War defences. Twentieth-century expansion behind Holywell Street has created fine new relaxed quadrangles, and the new library of 1977, faced in concrete and glass, is a major addition to Oxford's contemporary architecture.

194 FAR LEFT *The severe façade to Parks Road, with the gate tower 1610*

195 BELOW *The spacious square quadrangle of three storeys, with chapel, left, and dining hall, right, separated by a frontispiece of orders. The symmetry in planning is unrelenting and even demands a false door (right) and two decorative louvres*

196 LEFT *The centrepiece (1613) with four orders of architecture. The founder, Nicholas Wadham, holding a model of his College, and Dorothy his wife who saw it built, stand below James I. The tracery of the window is typical of the period and sums up the nature of Oxford's early seventeenth-century design*

197 The interior of the dining hall in the best Jacobean manner, with a fine, brash hammer-beam roof and good contemporary woodwork in the screen and cresting

198 A detail of the antechapel, with the excellent monument of Sir John Portman (1624)

Worcester College

The purchase of the impoverished Gloucester Hall by the trustees of Sir Thomas Cooks in 1714 resulted in the development of Worcester College. The site was that of the long-dissolved Benedictine Gloucester College, of which considerable ranges of buildings still survived. The central block, designed by George Clarke, with advice from Nicholas Hawksmoor, was begun in 1720, and has formed the termination of Beaumont Street since the 1820s. The block is ingeniously planned, the central entrance and lodge between the dining hall and chapel, with the first-floor library above and behind over an open arcade. From the arcade, the sharp contrast between the fifteenth-century monastic camerae to the left and the long north range in plain eighteenth-century Classical, may be enjoyed. Beyond, the fine gardens contain a lake, and the Oxford Canal skirts the boundary.

199 The eighteenth-century central block facing Beaumont Street, designed by George Clarke and begun in 1720

200 *The interior of the elegant dining hall, decorated 1776–84 by James Wyatt, redecorated by William Burges in 1877 and remodelled back to Wyatt again this century*

201 *The remarkable interior of the chapel, designed by James Wyatt, but redecorated by William Burges in 1864 in a manner whch has given it a Neo-renaissance character of compelling power and interest*

202 RIGHT *Wyatt's ceiling of 1783 to the chapel is intact, but almost lost under Burges' superb redecoration of 1864*

203 ABOVE *The elegant interior of the first-floor library room, completed 1734–6. The plain ceiling and painted woodwork make a striking contrast to the other show-room libraries, but the arrangement of books along the walls is confirmed*

204 FAR LEFT *A detail of the figures on the central marble candlestick-lectern is by Thomas Nicholls, dated 1865*

205 TOP LEFT *A detail of a choir-stall bench-end with one of the thirty-four creatures represented (which include a dodo)*

206 LEFT *The beautiful spiral stone staircase rising to the library, with a light wrought-iron balustrade*

207 *Worcester contains remarkable survivals of its monastic predecessor in the long range of medieval camerae. Each block served a separate monastery. The picturesque appearance of these is seen here from the garden*

208 *The Provost's Lodgings, 1773–6, by Henry Keene, from the garden, with the earlier block of the College behind*

Some Late Nineteenth- and Twentieth-Century College and Hall Foundations

The growth of the reformed University of Oxford has seen a corresponding growth in the buildings, to serve changing needs. Theological, Nonconformist and Roman Catholic institutions, together with halls for women undergraduates have become established and flourish in Oxford. The halls for women have developed as colleges and they have been followed by an explosion of new college foundations, such as St. Peter's, Nuffield, St. Catherine's and Wolfson. Architecturally, these recent institutions either use converted residential property, or have created new complexes of buildings, or occupy a mixture of both old and new. Many of the new buildings are of considerable distinction but, as befits our age of uncertainty, are designed in diverse styles from the International-Modern to Victorian-Edwardian revival.

209 Lady Margaret Hall, Norham Gardens. The Wolfson Quadrangle is a surprise after the blank entrance façade. The centre-piece, Talbot, was designed by Reginald Blomfield in 1909, but the quadrangle was completed only in 1961 by Raymond Erith, whose library stands to the left

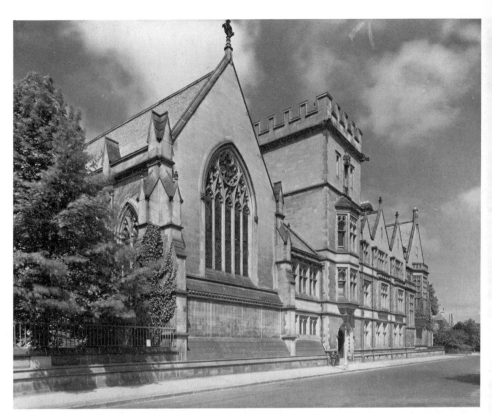

174

210 LEFT *Manchester College (not a formal University college), Mansfield Road, 1891–3, by Thomas Worthington*

211 Mansfield College (a permanent private hall of the University), Mansfield Road. The college group from the south with, right, the chapel and, centre, the dining hall, designed by Basil Champneys, 1887–9

212 ABOVE *The charming dining hall at Mansfield College with a touch of William Burges' fairy-tale medieval*

213 The excellent galleried library at Mansfield College, decorated very much in the tradition of William Morris

214 LEFT *Nuffield College, New Road. Founded by W. R. Morris, Lord Nuffield, in 1937 and built 1949–60 to the designs of Harrison, Barnes and Hubbard. The inner quadrangle is divided by a formal canal and the new tower and spire is a welcome addition to the skyline*

215 TOP *The plain interior of the Nuffield dining hall, with a massive fireplace to warm the high table*

216 Pusey House. The superb choir of the chapel of the Anglican theological institute in St. Giles, designed by Temple Moore, 1911–14. The altar, ciborium and glass by Sir Ninian Comper, 1937

217 ABOVE *St. Anne's College, Woodstock Road. The central block of 1938 by Giles Gilbert Scott*

218 RIGHT *St. Antony's College, Woodstock Road. The Old Building was built, for the society of the Holy Trinity, by Charles Buckeridge in 1866–8*

219 *The oldest building taken over by St. Hilda's is an Oxford rarity, a small eighteenth-century mansion. Built about 1780 in the Adam manner and recently carefully restored*

220 *St. Hilda's College, Cowley Place. The southern block of college houses, with the absorbed and much extended Cowley Grange of 1877 by William Wilkinson, left, and Alison and Peter Smithson's strange Garden Building of 1968–70, right, enjoy a beautiful park-like setting by the Cherwell*

221 *St. Hugh's College, St. Margaret's Road. The entrance block and lodges are a rosy Neo-Georgian; by Buckland and Haywood, 1914–16*

222 *Somerville College, Woodstock Road. A fine, spacious central garden is flanked on the north side by the library of 1903 designed by Basil Champneys*

The Modern Setting

223 *Ancient and Modern together 1978. The centre of the City of Oxford seen from the western hills at Raleigh Park, with the village of North Hinksey and the Ring Road in the foreground*

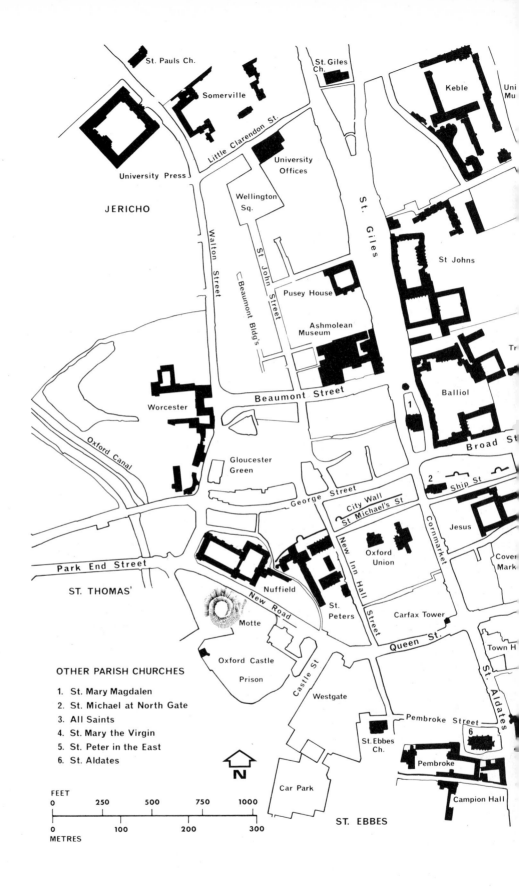

St. Pauls Ch.

Somerville

St. Giles Ch.

Keble

Uni Mu

Little Clarendon St.

University Offices

St. Giles

Wellington Sq.

JERICHO

University Press

St John Street

Beaumont Bldg's

Pusey House

St Johns

Walton Street

Ashmolean Museum

Balliol

1

Broad St

Worcester

Beaumont Street

Oxford Canal

Gloucester Green

2

Ship St

George Street

City Wall

Jesus

St. Michael's St

Cornmarket

Cover Mark

Park End Street

Oxford Union

New Inn Hall Street

ST. THOMAS'

Nuffield

New Road

Oxford Castle
Prison

St. Peters

Carfax Tower

Town H

Motte

Queen St.

Castle St

OTHER PARISH CHURCHES

1. St. Mary Magdalen

2. St. Michael at North Gate

3. All Saints

4. St. Mary the Virgin

5. St. Peter in the East

6. St. Aldates

St. Aldates

Westgate

Pembroke Street

6

St. Ebbes Ch.

Pembroke

N

Campion Hall

FEET

| 0 | 250 | 500 | 750 | 1000 |

Car Park

0   100   200   300

METRES

ST. EBBES

Plan of Oxford

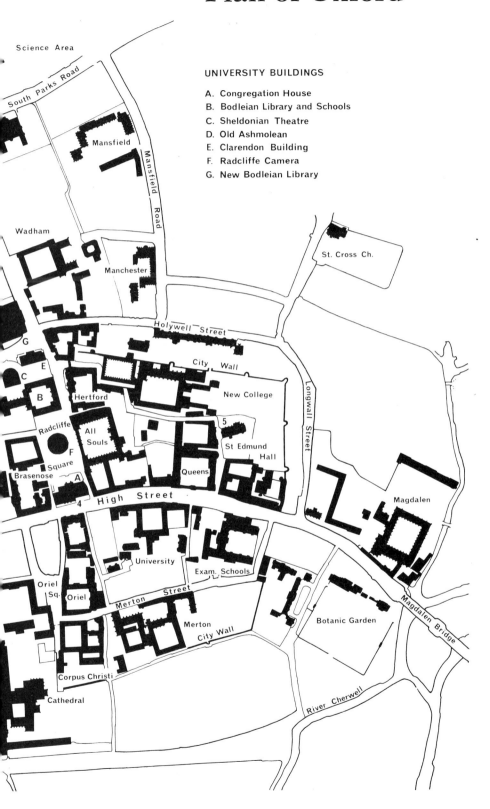

UNIVERSITY BUILDINGS

A. Congregation House
B. Bodleian Library and Schools
C. Sheldonian Theatre
D. Old Ashmolean
E. Clarendon Building
F. Radcliffe Camera
G. New Bodleian Library

Select Bibliography for further reading

ARKELL, W. J. *Oxford Stone* Faber, 1947; S. R., Wakefield, 1970.

CURL, J. S. *The Erosion of Oxford* Oxford Illustrated Press, 1977.

GREEN, V. H. H. *A History of Oxford University* Batsford, 1974.

MORRIS, J. *Oxford* Faber, 1965; Oxford 1978.

OAKESHOTT, W. F. *Oxford Stone Restored 1957–1974* Oxford, 1975.

PEVSNER, N. and SHERWOOD, J. *The Buildings of England: Oxfordshire* Penguin, 1974.

ROYAL COMMISSION ON HISTORICAL MONUMENTS IN ENGLAND *An Inventory of the Historical Monuments in the City of Oxford* H.M.S.O., 1939.

SHARP, T. *Oxford Replanned* Architectural Press, 1948, for Oxford City Council.

WOOLLEY, A. R. *The Clarendon Guide to Oxford* Oxford, 1979.

Christ Church College Meadow

Charwell

Christ Church Coll. new walkes

50

The Bowling Green

Magdalen College Grove

A Bowling Green